LESSONS
LEARNED

LESSONS LEARNED

Stories from a Lifetime of Organizing

ARNIE GRAF

LESSONS LEARNED
Stories from a Lifetime of Organizing
by Arnie Graf

Edited by Gregory F. Augustine Pierce
Cover and text design and typesetting by Patricia A. Lynch

Copyright © 2020 by Arnie Graf

Published by ACTA Publications, 4848 N. Clark Street,
Chicago, IL 60640, (800) 397-2282, www.actapublications.com

Library of Congress Number: 2020945913
ISBN: 978-0-87946-688-6
Printed in the United States of America by Total Printing Systems
Year 35 34 33 32 31 30 29 28 27 26 25 24 23 22 21 20
Printing 20 19 18 17 16 15 14 13 12 11 10 9 8 7 6 5 4 3 2 First

♲ Text printed on 30% post-consumer recycled paper.

CONTENTS

....

Dedication

To Lucile

INTRODUCTION

....

Thirty years ago, I received an invitation from Bishop Desmond Tutu to go to South Africa and conduct training in organizing for community and religious leaders in that country. The invitation came through Trinity Church in New York City. In the previous decade, Trinity had quietly supported Bishop Tutu by funding visits to the United States for clergy and lay leaders from South Africa who were engaged in the struggle to overthrow the apartheid regime there. Those leaders arrived in New York and one of the things they always did was observe the organizing and affordable home building efforts of one of our IAF affiliates, East Brooklyn Congregations.

Once apartheid crumbled, Bishop Tutu thought it might be the right time for the IAF to go to South Africa. So he conveyed that invitation to Trinity Church in New York City, and the good people at Trinity passed it along to my colleague, Mike Gecan, and me. We accepted immediately.

As I prepared for the trip, I did what every traveler would do—assemble the clothes and other items that would be needed during a three-week period away from home. But I also reviewed and then "packed" some other items—the concepts, tools, and training sessions I had conducted for 20 years as an Industrial Areas Foundation organizer in the United States.

So, what were those concepts, universal principles, and habits of thought—tested in many ways once we were in South Africa and working with 50 leaders there? Developed over the years and refined and adjusted regularly ever since, they are the basis for this book.

The first of these is an understanding that a healthy society depends on the functioning of three healthy, even robust, sectors—a <u>market sector</u>, a <u>governmen</u>tal or state sector, and a <u>voluntary or civic sector</u>. We were getting ready to fly into a country that had been utterly dominated by an oppressive and violent state sector: the apartheid state. In our country today, it's the market sector that dominates. But in both apartheid South Africa then and in America now, the third sector was under siege and much diminished.

The French writer Alexis de Tocqueville, who visited the United States of America in the early nineteenth century, observed that Americans achieved the common good primarily through voluntary associations. "In every case," he said, "as the head of any new undertaking, where in France you would find the government or in England some territorial mandate, in the United States you are sure to find an association."

In South Africa, the clergy and civic leaders of the third sector were systematically targeted for arrest, torture, and even death because the apartheid government correctly understood that those leaders were a threat to a totalitarian state. In the U.S., there has been little deliberate targeting but, rather, a 30-year period of gradual hollowing out and decline. The growing vacuum in our voluntary sector that is occurring in our congregations, unions, and associations has in large part led to the dangerous polarization of our entire society we are experiencing today.

The growing vacuum in our voluntary sector has led in part to the dangerous polarization of our entire society.

This phenomenon has been accelerating at warp speed due to the overwhelming use of social media. Although the Internet has created many remarkable and exciting advancements, it is not a substitute for face to face contact, without which relationships are narrowly confined and will either wither or die. In my opinion, this is why so many social justice organizations that are formed over social media seem to have a short life span.

While a good deal of blame for our weakening democracy is rightly placed on the outsized power of the market and political sectors, too little attention is focused on our fragmented civic sector. Many wounds to the civic sector have been self-inflicted: a penchant for bureaucratic rather than relational approaches and a tendency to drift into partisan activities. The reality of these wounds leaves too much space for the unaccountable market and political players to operate in. (For more on this phenomenon, see Mike Gecan's book *People's Institutions in Decline*.)

To address this imbalance of power, people in the U.S. organize a vast array of movements and organizations. My engagement in public life came as a naïve nineteen-year-old with the Congress of Racial Equality (CORE) that was founded by James Farmer. CORE was one of the major civil rights organizations that operated during the 1960s.

While working with CORE, I experienced the

fears and exhilarations of a powerful movement that won many important victories; however, I also experienced the frustration in working to mobilize and re-mobilize people time and again. As Doctor Charles Payne, in his wonderful book *I've Got the Light of Freedom* says, "The community mobilizing tradition is founded on large scale, relatively short-term public events."

Doctor Payne points out that there is another tradition. It resides not in mobilization, but in community organization. This lineage, "...comes with a different sense of what freedom means, and therefore places a greater emphasis on long term development of leadership in ordinary men and women." Payne notes that if Dr. Martin Luther King, Jr., represented the best idea of mobilizing, then Ella Baker, one of the founders of the civil rights movement, best embodied the tradition of community organizing.

Not that it is a question of pitting movement against community organizing, because both are necessary and important; however, without the development of a robust civic sector involving both, our democracy will continue to fray as our market and public sector gain more power without accountability.

For over forty years, I have worked with the Industrial Areas Foundation (IAF), founded by Saul Alinsky in 1940 to organize city, county, and metropolitan-wide non-partisan, institutionally based community organizations throughout the country. These "affiliates" of the IAF knit together multi-faith congregations, synagogues, mosques, and temples with local unions and various civic organizations and not-for-profit associations to amass enough power to both challenge and engage the corporate and political leaders in the geography in which they are based.

These organizations, at their best, have forced changes in laws and redirected large sums of money from city, county, and state governments to address decades of neglect. Additionally, some of these organizations have developed innovative ways to address what formerly seemed like impossible problems to overcome. For example, East Brooklyn Congregations (EBC) in New York City developed ways to physically rebuild entire blighted neighborhoods by developing over five thousand affordable homes that moderate- and low-income people could afford and did purchase. In 1994, Baltimore United in Leadership Development (BUILD) successfully forced the city of Baltimore to pass the first Living Wage law in the country.

And in San Antonio, Texas, Communities Organized for Public Service (COPS) changed the entire political dynamic of the city. The relentless work of COPS over the years forced the spending of one *billion* dollars on building a drainage system so people who lived in Mexican-American neighborhoods did not have to live with the fear of the floods that regularly ruined their homes and too often took the lives of their children. Additionally, due to COPS' organizing, the city built innumerable parks, playgrounds, libraries, and many other neighborhood facilities.

The COPS organization was instrumental in winning a referendum that reformed the composition of the city council. This victory changed the way candidates running for a city council position were elected by requiring voting for city council candidates by single districts rather than having all members of the council run citywide (thereby diluting the impact of Latino communities.) In the first election for city council members after the referendum passed, the composition of the council changed from seven Anglo council members, two Mexican American members, and one African-American member to five Mexican American members, one African-American member, and four Anglo members. This meant the first major-Texas city that was majority Mexican American now had fair ethnic representation on the city council—a harbinger of emerging Latino political power and elected representation throughout the state.

This victory changed the way candidates running for a city council position were elected.

These are just a few examples of the important social, economic, and political changes that powerful

IAF organizations have created. I could go on, but if you want to read more firsthand stories like these, told by leaders and organizers on the front lines of social justice, get a copy of *Reveille for a New Generation: Organizers and Leaders Reflect on Power*, compiled and edited by Greg Pierce, which contains an excerpt from the book you have in your hands.

Note: Chapter One of my book is devoted to describing some of the basic universal principles that successful community organizations follow to build and maintain power. In Chapters 2-5, you will find stories from five organizations based in different cities across the United States that illustrate many of these universals. Chapter 6 describes my experience working for the U.K. Labour Party from 2011-2013 and how in England citizens and party leaders employed some of these basic political concepts to win an election in a large County Council race that had been previously controlled by the Tories.

ONE

SOME ORGANIZING ESSENTIALS

I have chosen to include in this book five stories from organizations I worked for that were in different stages of development but successfully utilized many of what the Industrial Areas Foundation (IAF) regards as "universals." Although the membership bases of the 60-plus IAF affiliates around the country and in a few other countries vary greatly, these principles remain the same wherever the IAF is working today. The list of universals I have chosen to describe is by no means exhaustive; however, in combing through my notes and the workshops that my colleagues and I have taught over the years, I have chosen those I feel are essential for anyone trying to do this kind of organizing to understand.

The first principle is the reality and importance of power. Period. Full stop. A. Phillip Randolph (founder of the Brotherhood of Sleeping Car Porters, the architect of the Poor People's Campaign, and one of the leaders of the 1963 Civil Rights March on Washington, DC) clearly stated that power is the reason for building any broad-based organization:

> At the banquet table of nature, there are no reserved seats. You get what you can take and you keep what you can hold. If you cannot take anything, you won't get anything. And if you can't hold anything, you won't keep anything without an organization.

The word *power*, for many people, is filled with multiple negative connotations because they themselves have at times been treated abusively by those in power. I believe this is a case of guilt by association, because the root meaning of the word *power* is simply "the ability to act." Under that definition, power is a very positive quality, especially for people who are being ignored, oppressed, or—yes—abused by those who have it.

Sometimes when I begin a workshop on power, I do a word association. I call out the word "power" and ask for the participants to respond by calling out the first name of a person that comes to their mind. Frequently, the participants call out names of people for whom they have a strong dislike, e.g., dictators, local politicians or corporate leaders, sometimes their own boss, etc. When I ask them, however, if they are glad that President Lincoln, Doctor King, Gandhi, or some other political leader had power, they invariably say a resounding, "yes."

Many people bring up historian Lord Acton's famous saying, "Power tends to corrupt and absolute power corrupts absolutely." (Acton was a Catholic lay leader in England, who was speaking about the Vatican of his time.) I first remind them of the word *tends* in the first part of the Acton quote. Then I quote Rollo May from *Power and Innocence*, who said: "Far from treating power only as a term of abuse, one which is applied to our enemies (i.e., they are power driven, but we are motivated only by benevolence, reason, and morality), I use *power* as a description of a fundamental aspect of the life process.... If we neglect the factor of power, as is the tendency in our day of reaction against the destructive effects of the misuse of power, we shall lose values that are essential to our existence as human." Or, as Edgar D. Friedenberg said it: "All weakness tends to corrupt, and impotence corrupts absolutely." After I lay out these dueling quotes, a great discussion generally ensues about the meaning and good use of power.

By the way, I strongly challenge those who insist they want power for their community leaders but not for themselves. That kind of *noblesse oblige* is patronizing and unacceptable. Everyone should want power. The question of power is not whether it is good or bad. The reality is that without power we can neither defend against injustices nor initiate new solutions to overcome those injustices. Dr. King said:

> Power properly understood is the ability to achieve purpose. It is the strength required to bring about social, political, or economic changes. In this sense, power is not only

desirable but necessary in order to implement the demands of love and justice. One of the greatest problems in history is that the concepts of love and power are usually contrasted as polar opposites. Love is identified with a resignation of power and power with a denial of love. What is needed is a realization that power without love is reckless and abusive, and that love without power is sentimental and anemic. Power at its best is love implementing the demands of justice. Justice at its best is love correcting everything that stands against love.

The question is how you get power and how you use it.

So, the question is not whether power is good or evil; the questions are how you get it and what you do with it. There are a limited number of ways to get power (at least in the secular world). If you have wealth and choose to use it to influence political, financial, and/or social change, you have power. If you have attained a certain status—for example, you are a CEO of major corporation, a mayor, a governor, or hold some other position, such as chairperson of the chamber of commerce, leader of a religious denomination, etc.—you have power.

Given that most people have neither great wealth nor major status, however, if they want power they must organize their own people and/or money so that they can deliver them consistently and persistently. That is the IAF answer to the question, "How do people's institutions exercise power?"

An understanding and appreciation of what the IAF calls "self-interest"—your own, your allies', your opponents'—is the second universal principle. If we are to amass and keep power, we must understand people's self-interest. Unfortunately, the concept of self-interest, like that of power, has a negative connotation for many people because they equate it with *selfishness*. It's not. In fact, in many ways self-interest is the opposite of selfishness. Building a powerful organization requires an understanding of people's different and multiple self-interests. A successful movement, while containing multiple aspects, usually organizes around a single area of interest: for example, the Civil Rights movement, the Women's movement, the Environmental movement, etc. A broad-based organization of the kind the IAF tries to build organizes through peoples' varied and multiple interests in an attempt to knit together a wide spectrum of interests. This approach requires a good deal of trust and ongoing negotiations between people who have different interests.

While the word *selfish* means "...of a person, action, or motive lacking consideration of others." The word *self-interest*, on the other hand, when "interest" is broken down to its Latin roots *"inter"* (between) and *"esse"* (to be), means literally "to be between." *That is, our self-interest is not only what we want, it is the common good that exists between ourselves and others.*

A person's self-interest is essentially comprised of two drives. The first component is the drive for self-preservation (for example, food, shelter, safety).

The second drive is for recognition and meaning. A vivid example of this took place in Memphis 1968 during the sanitation worker's strike. The placards on the front and the back that the strikers wore on their bodies on the picket lines did not say, "We want better wages," although they certainly deserved higher wages. The placards simply said, "I am a man."

Without an understanding of a person's multiple self-interests, organizers and leaders will make numerous mistakes, whether dealing with a business, a politician, the media, a non-governmental not-for-profit, or even the very people in the people's institutions they are trying to organize.

The third universal principle that becomes a habit if practiced regularly is a commitment to organize "relational power." In IAF, this means using one-to-one meetings as a primary tool. A face-to-face (or in the time of pandemic a zoom to zoom) meeting between two people for 30-45 minutes is the best way to initiate the beginnings of a relationship and to begin to discern each person's self-interest. This type of meeting will let you know if you want to pursue a follow up meeting.

Over time, if a relationship deepens, your understanding of why both sides act and think in certain ways (their deepest self-interests) will reveal itself through the stories they tell about themselves as well as those you share about yourself. A person's self-interest (like your own) is not static. This is true not only **A person's** for people we are trying to orga-**self-interest is** nize but for allies and opponents **not static.** as well. When leaders and organizers stereotype people, we can miss opportunities to challenge them or to negotiate with them in new ways. The kind of thinking that stems from ideology or prejudice limits an organization's prospects for success.

Organizing around self-interest and its changing nature means there are no permanent allies nor permanent enemies. What your organization has are permanent interests. This can be difficult to negotiate with a person in power who has either steadfastly refused to recognize the organization, publicly disrespected the organization, or literally tried to destroy the organization (for example, trying to cut off the funds that foundations, corporations, or individuals donate). Here is one example of how this universal worked in this situation in Maryland.

Throughout most of the 1980s, William Donald Schaefer, then mayor of Baltimore City, Maryland, did all he could to destroy the IAF affiliate Baltimorians United in Leadership Development (BUILD). He maintained this stance until he was elected governor. For a guy like Schaefer, you were either for him or against him. His deep dislike and distrust of BUILD, over time, was mirrored by the attitude of the organization towards him, though its leaders always recognized they had to deal with him.

In 1986, however, Mayor Schaefer ran successfully for the office of governor of Maryland. The following year, his hand-picked candidate to replace him as mayor, Clarence Burns, lost a close election to Kurt Schmoke. Because of this, Schaefer lost much of his control over the city. Governor Schaefer believed, correctly or incorrectly, that BUILD's non-partisan get-out-the-vote campaign was partially responsible for Schmoke's victory, and this belief solidified his deep animosity towards the organization.

Early in Schaefer's term as governor, however, because of various pressures applied by representatives, senators, and various organizations from around the state, he pushed several anti-gun laws through the legislature. This set off a very expensive and successful campaign by pro-gun advocates, including the NRA, to gain enough citizen's signatures to force a referendum to overthrow the newly passed gun-control laws. To defeat the referendum, Governor Schaefer needed a large voter turnout from Baltimore; however, he had a problem because of his poor relationship with Mayor Schmoke. This meant he had difficulty coordinating his efforts with those of the mayor. This situation presented BUILD with a political opportunity to change the nature of their relationship with Governor Schaefer.

There were two problems BUILD faced in taking advantage of this potential opening. First, the organization had not worked for the passage of the anti-gun legislation in the legislature. At the time, the organization's efforts were largely focused on education and housing. Second, the organization had no desire to assist Governor Schaefer just to save his legislation. BUILD already had a good relationship with Mayor Schmoke and was doing important business with him. Additionally, some of the leaders believed that if Governor Schaefer failed to prevail on the gun issue, perhaps he would see the need to rethink his relationships with BUILD, Mayor Schmoke, and others with whom he had refused to work in the past.

BUILD's antipathy toward Governor Schaefer ran deep. To take advantage of this possible opening to ally with Governor Schaefer was an anathema to many of the organization's leaders. Numerous long and emotional conversations amongst the leaders took place. Eventually, they began to reflect on the universal principle that the organization should not have either permanent enemies or permanent allies, only permanent interests. The leaders reminded themselves that they would need the state government, now headed by Schaefer, to provide the low market financing for the one thousand homes it hoped to build for moderate-to-low-income families to own.

The leaders decided to meet with Mark Wasserman, a man who was at the time the new governor's chief of staff. The leaders told Wasserman that the organization would work to defeat the referendum to overturn the gun-control legislation. BUILD leaders told Wasserman the organization would work separately from the state but make public the precincts in which it planned to turn out enough voters to defeat the referendum. The organization conducted a large and visible get-out-the-vote campaign. The referendum was in fact defeated, and BUILD's campaign was duly noted by the media, as well as by Schaefer's staff and supporters, including Mark Wasserman.

A few weeks after the successful campaign, the governor invited twenty-five major players and organizations who he deemed were the most influential in defeating the referendum to a celebratory dinner. On the list was BUILD. The organization sent Carol Reckling, a major BUILD leader to the dinner. This was the breakthrough the organization had been looking for.

A year later, Governor Schaefer agreed to assist BUILD's effort to develop one thousand homes for sale to first-time homeowners by making 12.2 million dollars of low-interest money available. More important for recognition's sake, the governor came to St. Peter Claver Catholic Church, which belonged to BUILD and was located in the neighborhood where the proposed housing was to take place to make this announcement. There Schaefer publicly shook hands with BUILD leaders in front of over five hundred members and the media.

The fourth universal principle I want to raise up is the discipline of distinguishing between a problem and an issue. A problem is almost by definition general and large and therefore hard to act successfully upon. An issue, according to IAF training, is immediate, specific, and something an organization has enough power to legitimately have a chance of winning. Bad housing in an inner-city neighborhood, for example, is an intractable *problem*. Systematic redlining of a minority community by banks, though, can be a potentially winnable *issue* with an effective strategy that uses the power an organization has at the time.

Given the grievous and unjust nature of refusing to lend money to Black or Hispanic families, furthermore, an organization can polarize its anger towards a specific bank and can personalize its action on the bank's president. The organization can dramatize with stories to paint the bank as one hundred percent wrong. This leaves no gray area between right and wrong, even though in life few things are one hundred percent right or one hundred percent wrong. Without this kind of polarization, people will not turn out in the numbers and with the energy to act persistently and consistently in the manner that is required to win. But if and when the actions taken by an organization lead to a victory, it is also important to depolarize and de-personalize. Today's opponent may be tomorrow's ally.

The distinction between a problem and an issue is often the difference between defeat and winning.

Once the negotiations begin between the opposition and the organization, the organization will win as much as it has the power to compel. The distinction between a problem and an issue is often the difference between defeat and winning, even if you only win fifty percent of the organization's initial demands. (See the next chapter in this book for a more detailed example of how this universal worked with COPS in San Antonio.)

In my younger organizing days, I participated in (and even organized) far too many demonstrations that gathered large numbers of people—albeit filled with anger, energy, and hope—only to see the participants disperse after forty minutes of speeches. We had no power analysis, no clear target, and no next step announced. We in the IAF consider such demonstrations to be "protests"—what groups often do when they don't really have any power. We prefer "actions."

The word *action* refers to what an organization decides to do tactically once it has landed on an issue to take on or advance. And that means we should focus on our fifth and final universal principle: the use of public *action* to get a *reaction*. Alinsky taught, "The action is in the reaction" and said the first reaction that is necessary for an organization is to gain recognition. Without recognition, it cannot negotiate, because publicly it does not exist in the eyes of its opponent. This is the first hurdle every union or community organization faces.

For example, for a number of years I worked with the Greater Boston Interfaith Organization (GBIO) (see Chapter 5). For most of those years, Mayor Thomas Menino refused to recognize GBIO. In fact, if he did mention the organization, he ridiculed it by calling it "The Greater Boston Idiot's Organization." Similar to the story about Mayor Schaefer in Baltimore, it took a number of years of consistent power building, including making an ally of Governor Mitt Romney to get a form of universal healthcare passed through the Massachusetts state legislature before Mayor Menino began to negotiate with GBIO in any meaningful way.

There are many ways for community organizations and unions to get a reaction from people in power. Oftentimes the organization must create tension in order to get a reaction. This is because tension creates uncomfortable feelings that often cause people to react in ways they would not normally do.

Tension often causes leaders to feel as uncomfortable as it makes their opponents, so the leaders are often reluctant to initiate it. However, it is important for them to learn and remember that in the public arena, respect is more important than being liked.

For many people, this is easier said than done. It takes a good deal of training and experience for leaders and organizers to devise and run effective public actions that elicit reactions that can lead to future actions.

The actual reaction you get will lead to the formation of the next action. Often direct confrontation is an effective way to elicit such a reaction; however, it is not the only way to do so. Sometimes humor, or a story, or silence, or ridicule does a better job of creating a useful reaction. (See Chapter 3 for an extended example.) The point is not to be predictable. Do not mistake activity for action. Repeating the same tactics over and over will not elicit a reaction from your adversary.

Of course, no matter how thoughtfully an organization attempts to create a plan to get a reaction, it often gets something very different; however, the actual reaction you do get will lead to the formation of the next action. Remember, the action is in the reaction. No matter what, getting no reaction at all is the worst outcome of any action. Trust me on this!

After every action, the organizer and the leaders should immediately conduct a 15-20 minute evaluation. The purpose for this quick evaluation is to allow people to express their feelings in real time and imagine potential next steps. After a large or particularly important action, IAF organizations conduct a more in-depth evaluations for a larger group of leaders at a later but timely convenient place. Here people can express their feelings after a week of ruminating about what happened at the action and discuss both the important things they learned and decide on their next steps. During these longer evaluations (which are really training sessions as well), leaders get the opportunity to hold themselves accountable in regard to turnout and performance: Did they get the reaction they had planned for? If not, then the next question is, why not? The answer to these and other questions leads to the discussion of what actions need to take place to reach their goals.

The universals I have described in this chapter are by no means *all* the principles that are important for leaders and organizers to learn, but they are in my opinion the *most critical* to know and practice. And, of course, even the universals must be examined given the setting you are in.

Once we arrived in South Africa, for example, Mike Gecan and I had to re-think each of these principles in the context of a crumbling racist totalitarian society. We had to redo how we taught individual meetings because, at that time in that country, how would you know if you were talking to an informant?) Or, more immediately, in the midst of a coronavirus pandemic, how can you do one-to-one relational meetings if you cannot meet with people face-to-face?

With this caveat, I hope you will be able to appreciate these basic universal principles—ones that IAF leaders and organizers have developed and put into action—as they are fleshed out in the following chapters.

TWO

....

COPS VS. EDF

I n 1976, I moved with my family from Milwaukee, where I had been organizing with the Industrial Areas Foundation (IAF) for five years, to San Antonio to become the second lead organizer of Committees Organized for Public Services (COPS).

COPS was the first of the modern IAF affiliates, which is what we call our institutionally-based organizations. (Any not-for-profit "people's institution" that is primarily owned and essentially run by their members can join an IAF affiliate.) A large percentage of these "people's institutions" are churches, synagogues, mosques, and temples, and the rest are mostly local unions, civic associations, not-for-profit service providers, and neighborhood organizations. We build them into the kind of power organization that the IAF has created in the period following Saul

Alinsky's death and the emergence of Ed Chambers as the IAF national executive director. The IAF is now organized into Metro IAF and Southwest IAF, with over 60 affiliates. (including organizations in the UK, Canada, Germany, and Australia.)

When Ed Chambers, Alinsky's successor, asked me to consider moving to San Antonio, I was simultaneously flattered and challenged. I was flattered because COPS was far and away the most successful organization affiliated with the IAF at the time. The organization had over 30 Catholic parishes and one Protestant church as members throughout the Mexican American sections of the city—organized by a brilliant and driven organizer named Ernesto Cortes. I had gotten to know Ernie Cortes when he spent six weeks with me in Milwaukee. He came there to do a power analysis of the Latino community. I had never met anyone as intelligent and well-read as Ernie.

My uncertainty about moving to San Antonio centered around the fact that I am an Anglo who does not speak Spanish. Further, being Jewish, I knew very little about the Catholic Church and the local parishes that comprised 95% of COPS membership. Finally, I did not know if I was in Ernie's league as an organizer. I had built good organizations in Milwaukee, but nothing compared to COPS.

When I decided to go to San Antonio to be interviewed for the lead organizer position, I was met by very skeptical leaders. Some did not show up for their interview with me. Many others made it clear to me that they did not want Ernie to leave to go to Los Angeles to organize there. After a couple of days, I met with Ernie to say that I was returning to Milwaukee. I told him that the leaders were clearly not ready for him to be replaced.

There were two things that stuck in my mind on my way back to Milwaukee. First, the passion of the COPS' leaders I met was deep and abiding; second, I could not erase what I had seen as Cortes took me through the Mexican American neighborhoods.

The closest place I had ever experienced to what I saw in those neighborhoods of San Antonio was the village where I had lived in Sierra Leone in my twenties as a Peace Corp volunteer in West Africa. Both places lacked paved streets and sidewalks, and neither place had a drainage system. The streets in the Mexican American communities were lined with dugout trenches to catch the rainwater that flowed heavily during the frequent flash floods. When the heavy rains came, the trenches overflowed with rushing water; and during these times, many children were either injured or drowned. These were the conditions faced by thousands of families in the tenth most populated city in the U.S. at the time.

A few months after I returned to Milwaukee, Ed Chambers again contacted me to see if I would be willing to return to San Antonio for a new round of interviews with the leaders. He said that the leaders were now prepared to see Cortes go to East Los

Angeles. Ernie confirmed this when I called him.

When I returned to San Antonio, I felt the leaders had accepted the fact that Ernie was going to L.A. I knew this because their interviews with me were very serious. After three days of intense interviews, I spent over an hour with all the primary leaders gathered so they could ask me any further questions that were on their minds. It was a good dynamic to be with thirty proven and trained leaders in a room and for them to experience me in front of them. I felt I had to show them the most authentic person I could be.

After excusing me from the room so they could talk among themselves, I was called back into the meeting room. They told me they had voted to hire me, and we settled on the date I would start. As we were about to go to the other end of the hall for some refreshments, one of the leaders stood up—looking as if he was in agony—and said "But this man is not of our faith!" As we walked over to get our refreshments, it was clear to me that the vote to hire me was anything but unanimous and that some of those seasoned Mexican American leaders were understandably skeptical.

During my first hectic year working for COPS, the organization averaged at least two local actions per week, along with regular city-wide actions and assemblies. Since the staff consisted of just me and Robert Rivera, the only COPS associate organizer at the time, many of the local actions were organized and led by local leaders. Sometimes neither Robert nor I even knew that some of these local actions had taken place until the leaders called and briefed us on the outcome.

By the second year of my tenure, a relationship of trust had solidified.

The leaders' energy and sense of ownership, which had been freed to express itself through COPS, continued to be kindled by the reactions they generated and the successes they experienced. By the second year of my tenure, a relationship of trust between the leaders and myself had solidified. Additionally, the relationship between me and some of the city insiders that Ernesto Cortes had introduced me to had also taken root.

One day, I received a call from a guy, let's call him Pete, who worked for the city planning department. Pete would call me periodically to inform me as to what was going on behind the scenes—decisions and activities he believed COPS should know about. He asked me to meet him late at night in a deserted spot where we would not be seen. Although I appreciated Pete's 's well-studied caution, this felt like something out of "deep throat" (from the movie about Watergate starring Robert Redford). It was around 11:00 pm when we met.

Pete kept looking nervously in every direction as we met, and his behavior raised a sense of anticipation and alarm in me. He made me swear that what he was about to tell me would never be traced back to him. This was always our agreement, so I was befuddled by his vociferous demand.

Pete then opened his briefcase and handed me a document by the Fantus Corporation, a major consulting firm that worked on behalf of cities throughout the country to determine their client's economic growth strategies. The Fantus Report had been commissioned by the Economic Development Corporation (EDF) of San Antonio. The EDF was the most politically influential organization in the city. Its membership consisted of the leading CEOs. Not much was known about the workings of the EDF by the public at the time. The chairman of the EDF was General Robert McDermott, the CEO of USAA Insurance Company—then and now an esteemed anchor corporation in the area.

Pete had placed paper clips on the pages he wanted to highlight. Since the report was very long, I asked him to give it to me so I could make a copy of it, but he refused to let it out of his sight, so I stood under a dim streetlight reading the portions of the report that Pete had selected. I was stunned by what I read.

The report stressed that San Antonio was a low-wage city. It went on to say that San Antonio had a highly-trainable, unskilled workforce and that the wages are lower than most sizeable industrial cities in Texas and around the country The report cited average hourly wages for the electronics industry nationally as \$4.90-\$5.06, while the average in San Antonio was a measly \$2.50-\$2.90. Besides touting the low wages in the electronics industry, the report noted that 75% of the employees in the textile and apparel industry were women. Furthermore, it stated that the apparel industry was a good fit for the city because Mexican Americans in general were docile and Mexican American women had nimble fingers. The report concluded that the EDF should "seek companies that will not disturb the present low wage scale."

San Antonio corporate leaders had vehemently denied that they had worked to block high-wage industries.

For years, San Antonio corporate leaders had vehemently denied that they worked to block high-wage industries from coming to San Antonio, even when past experience seemed to indicate that is exactly what they did. In the 1940s, according to former County Judge A.J. Pough, the San Antonio Chamber of Commerce had kept a Ford plant from locating in San Antonio. At the time, the Chamber had stated "Can't let Ford come in here. We got the Mexican element and cheap labor, and we can't afford to pay the wages they will bring." The Chamber went on to say that if Ford were allowed into San Antonio they would bring labor unions with them. They said that Ford had "sold us out!"

It was easy to understand why the EDF never wanted anyone to see the Fantus Report.

As I stood on that street corner with my nervous source and flipped through the pages of the report, I realized I was in a bind. Pete was adamant; he would not let the report out of his sight; however, he told me of a person who had another copy of the report, a person who liked and respected COPS, someone who might be willing to let me make a copy of the report.

I went home seething, with phrases like "docile workers" and "nimble fingers"—the strategy of deliberately suppressing an entire city's wages—running through my mind. I had to get my hands on the report so I could show it to the leaders.

The next day, I met with the person who Pete had told me was also in possession of the report. He was shocked that I knew of the report. I literally pleaded with him to give me the report so I could make a copy of it. I promised to return it to his office within two hours. Thankfully, after swearing to him several times that I would never divulge where I got the report, he gave it to me. I rushed to copy it and, within the promised two hours, returned the report to his office. No one to this day has ever found out where or how COPS got its hands on the Fantus Report.

The following day I met with Beatrice Gallego, then president of COPS. I gave her the report to read. When I returned to meet with her at the COPS office, she was livid. Ms. Gallego was a very smart and proud woman. I knew the report would set her on fire. She agreed that we would never mention who gave us the report. I then went to see Father Albert Benavides, COPS' most important clergy leader, so he could read the report. Fr. Al's reaction was predictably explosive. Within a few days, Ms. Gallego called the key leaders together to read the full report. We had the summary of the full report translated into Spanish for those leaders who were not comfortable reading it in English. After everyone read the summary, you could hear a pin drop.

The central question then was how could the COPS organization use the report to challenge the city's corporate leaders' cynical and long-concerted efforts to maintain San Antonio as a low-wage city? We began by meeting to analyze a typical Mexican American's family budget, itemizing the essentials, e.g., food, housing costs, clothing, utilities, etc. We then compared the leaders' cost of living to the average income of the families that lived in the Mexican American communities.

The disparity was stark. We found that in 1977

the average household income in the two predominantly Mexican American city council districts was $6,130.00. National government statistics showed at the time that urban families of four needed $16,236.00 "...just to maintain a moderate standard of living."

The leaders then listed and talked about what they did to make up for the gap. Some worked two and three jobs a day. They talked about not going to the dentist or doctor until a health condition became truly serious. Their diets lacked some essential foods. They often visited used clothing closets. From this discussion, each leader met with the core team leaders of their member institutions to present this analysis and discuss it. This organizing process took COPS a few weeks to complete. In the meantime, the leaders met to begin to map out a strategy.

The first step was to call the leaders of the core teams of our member parishes together. The outcome of that meeting was a decision to reach out to General

McDermott to set up a meeting with him. In the call we would let him know we had the Fantus Report and would release it at a press conference if he refused to meet with COPS.

Ms. Gallego and Fr. Benavides made the call, and I listened in. At first the General's secretary said he would be unavailable to meet in the next few months, as his schedule was jammed packed. She suggested we meet with one of the EDF's staff. Fr. Al told her this offer was totally unacceptable. He told her he would wait only two hours to hear whether or not General McDermott would agree to meet with the organization.

Within thirty minutes, the General himself called. He started by asking in an angry tone "Where did you get that report?" While he used civil language, his tone was the same as that of a politician confronted with an embarrassing photograph. Fr. Al replied in an equally angry tone that it did not matter where we got the report. He said that over 100 COPS leaders had read the report already and were furious. He told McDermott the report was disgraceful, patronizing, and racist. There was silence on the other end of the line. Fr. Al pressed, "Do you agree to meet or not!" Suddenly, the answer was a tension-filled "yes."

The meeting was scheduled for October 26, 1977, at 1:00 pm at Immaculate Heart of Mary Catholic Church, a downtown parish and COPS member. Fr. Al told McDermott that a team of leaders would meet with him first in a conference room and then he would be asked to go to the parish hall to meet with the membership to address his answers to COPS' two demands.

The first demand was to recall all of the Fantus reports that had been sent throughout the country with a clear and precise disclaimer regarding all of the contents in the report. The second demand was for the Chamber of Commerce to agree to focus on recruiting companies that paid their workers at least $15.00 per hour. (This was almost 40 years before Bernie Sanders made "fifteen bucks an hour" the center of his run for President.) We chose $15.00 per hour because that was the minimum required, even back then, for a family of four to live a decent life if one of them worked full time.

The leaders knew they would be attacked, not only by McDermott but by all the major corporate leaders, elected officials, and the media—in short by the entire political and business establishment of San Antonio. At best, COPS would be accused of being naïve, and at worst our leaders would be accused of destroying any hope of bringing any new business to San Antonio. But because the leaders wanted to provoke this argument about wages and what it took to raise a family in healthy and decent conditions, they decided to risk the attacks.

The leaders wanted to provoke this argument about wages and what it took to raise a family in healthy and decent conditions.

On the day of the action, at precisely 1:00 pm, over 500 COPS members packed the parish hall. The summary of the Fantus Report in English and Spanish was circulated, along with COPS' two demands. The membership had time to read the summary while the team of COPS leaders met with General McDermott in the parish conference room.

In the conference room, McDermott said that while some of the wording in the report left a lot to be desired, the strategy it called for was right. He told the leaders they had to be realistic. He said that since the city had a population with low education and skill levels, the EDF had to aim to recruit the appropriate businesses. The leaders, however, were having none of what the General was selling. He soon became agitated. "Did they know that the leading CEOs had paid for this very expensive report?" He said in no uncertain terms that trying to recruit businesses that paid $15.00 per hour was pure folly. The leaders asked him if he knew what it was like to try to raise a family on a minimum wage? Did he have a clue as to what it felt like to be described as a "docile" people?

At that point, the leaders ended the meeting and ushered General Robert McDermott to the parish hall to face the organization's membership

Fr. Benavides walked General McDermott to his podium, which was set up about ten feet from the COPS' podium. The 500 COPS leaders seemed to be inhaling and exhaling as one. They were disciplined, not docile; politically adroit, not manipulatable. The media cameras were clicking at a mile a minute, and the lights from the TV cameras lit up the hall.

Ms. Gallego introduced McDermott to complete silence (a very effective tactic but hard to organize). Then she introduced Fr. Al, and the hall erupted. McDermott looked stunned, like a general confronting an opposing army he had never experienced before. He did not know COPS. He had not bothered to do any research on us in preparation. When he had agreed to meet at 1:00 pm, he assumed that there would be 25 or 30 people present. He never expected to see over 500 people packed into a Catholic church hall.

From reading newspaper articles and watching local TV news, McDermott knew only that Fr. Benavides was popular, but he had no idea how brilliantly tough Fr. Al could be. General McDermott soon found out. After he tried to make his case to the membership, Fr. Al read aloud some of the most offending passages in the report in English and Spanish. He then asked McDermott why he approved of this report and allowed it to be sent out nationwide. Again the hall was silent. The TV cameras moved in to get McDermott's response. He looked lost. He kept trying to explain the EDF's good intentions. Fr. Al kept pressing him to apologize to COPS and the entire Mexican American community.

McDermott skirted making an apology and kept repeating how unreasonable and unrealistic the $15.00 per hour demand was. Fr. Al never let him off the hook. His replies to the General were met with loud cheers from the crowd. I had seen the brilliance of Fr. Al in action before, but I had never seen his total mastery on display like I did that day.

General McDermott, in that moment, because of Fr. Al's total command of the action, became the symbol of over 150 years of oppression of Mexican Americans. The only thing left for him to do was to bolt from the room—with the media in fast pursuit of him and the crowd roaring with pride and delight.

Someone stood on a chair and started chanting "Viva COPS." Many people joined in standing on their chairs—chanting and waving their COPS signs.

In organizing we talk about the tension between the world as it is and the world as it should be. We stress the need to operate on the ground, in reality, in the world as it is, but every once and a while there are moments where we see and feel the world as it should be. Seeing those non-docile leaders alive with joy, proud of their own history, full of admiration for their brilliant leaders—was such a moment for me, and I think for them too. In the years and decades that followed, many COPS leaders, before they passed away, stipulated that they be buried with their COPS buttons on their suits and dresses.

Over the next week, the leaders and I read, watched, and listened to the media coverage and interpretation of the action. For the most part, the coverage was positive; however, COPS was rebuked for its unrealistic $15.00 per hour demand.

One morning, about ten days after the action, I went outside my home to pick up the morning newspaper. As I opened the paper, I knew from the headline that we were in for a difficult time. The front-page headline and article reported that due to San Antonio's "bad business climate" the Allen-Bradley Company, which was based in Milwaukee, had decided not to relocate to San Antonio. This represented the loss of a major company and hundreds of jobs. When I went inside, every radio station ran this as the lead story. COPS was the villain. My phone was ringing nonstop—with leaders calling me in a state of panic.

You run an action to get a desired reaction that leads to a beneficial change; however, COPS was not the only organization that could run tough actions. Obviously, so could the EDF. A spokesman from Allen-Bradley was on all the radio stations saying that due to community "unrest" the company had removed San Antonio as a candidate for the place to which the company might relocate. These stories said that Allen-Bradley's hourly wage, although low, was higher than the average San Antonio wage. Over the next two days, COPS leaders were deluged with calls from people in the community, decrying the trouble and retribution the organization had caused.

It was remarkable how quickly many people from the community turned against the organization. Even some of the secondary leaders became very critical. It was as if, in two days, the roof had caved in.

It was remarkable how quickly many people from the community turned against the organization.

The COPS leaders quickly convened to assess the political damage and to forge a strategy. The first hour of the meeting was difficult and painful. The leaders had never experienced such emotional blowback from their own community. While up to that time COPS had not won every fight it had undertaken, eventually it had come out victorious. This appeared to be the first time that the organization would be knocked out cold.

The primary leaders and I experienced an hour of anxiety, fear, anger, and recriminations. Some of the leaders wanted the organization to settle for an apology from EDF because of its racist characterization of Mexican American people. They wanted the organization to drop the $15.00 per hour demand.

COPS, however, meant everything to many of the leaders. What felt like a crushing blow brought out people's fear that, without COPS, the old ways of the San Antonio's establishment's patronizing and blatant racism would return with impunity. After about an hour, Ms. Gallego, the COPS president, called for a break. She asked everyone to calm down and talk with one another for twenty minutes. While this took place, Ms. Gallego, Fr. Benavides, Mr. Andy Sarabia (COPS' first president), and I caucused to figure out how to proceed. When we reconvened, Ms. Gallego, Mr. Sarabia, and Fr. Benavides each gave brief talks asking the leaders to focus their anger on the EDF. Fr. Al asked the leaders what was wrong with calling on the EDF to make every effort to recruit companies that paid decent wages. He said he had grown up in the public housing projects in San Antonio and was sick and tired of working to scrape enough money together for his parishioners and neighbors to pay for essentials like rent, food, and money to see a doctor. He said he would never give up fighting for the dignity and decency good jobs would bring to people.

People believed in Fr. Benavides, and when he spoke about the peoples' struggles the room was totally transfixed on him. When he challenged the leaders to fight, people began speaking up. It seemed that everyone had found their voice. The meeting ended with renewed spirit.

When I arrived home after the meeting, I was thoroughly drained. I had experienced a wide range of emotions during the meeting—dread, fear, anger, hurt, and eventually solidarity. I kept playing over and over in my mind the mistakes I may have made. Did I push to go after the EDF too hard in COPS' relatively young life? Was it a mistake to call for a $15.00 per hour threshold? Was the action with General McDermott too harsh? Had I let a lot of people down by giving bad advice?

I got very little sleep that night.

The next day, I either spoke or met with Ms. Gallego, Mr. Sarabia, Fr. Benavides, and Ms. Carmen Badillo. I always touched base with Ms. Badillo. I had tremendous respect for her. She was not only filled with common sense; she always had her ear to the ground. Additionally, she was always honest with her thoughts and her feelings. She never hesitated to critique me, but always did so with care and support.

Carmen Badillo was not only filled with common sense; she always had her ear to the ground.

At the next meeting, COPS was back. The leaders were ready to go all out. They decided to hold a press conference to hit back at the EDF as hard as they could. The press conference began with some moving stories from a few leaders as to the hardships they had endured by working fulltime and still being in poverty. Ms. Gallego then called on the leadership of EDF to meet with the executive officers of COPS to develop an economic strategy that would benefit everyone in the city.

After the well-attended press conference, the COPS leaders flooded the Spanish-speaking talk radio stations and contacted leading newspaper columnists. The organization's strategy was to use this crisis to call on the EDF to work with COPS to end the low-wage strategy that had plagued the city for so long.

When General McDermott refused to respond to COPS call to meet, the media began to question his leadership. And we began to change the terms of the fight from the organization's demands for a $15 minimum wage and instead focused on the EDF's refusal to meet.

Because General McDermott had no appetite to meet, COPS no longer referred to the EDF by name. Everything was personalized to Robert McDermott himself. In action, it is very important to polarize on the issue and personalize on the person who has the decision-making authority. By personalizing our demands on McDermott, COPS replaced the amorphous EDF that few had ever heard of and placed all our pressure and tension on him as the symbol of the problem. Soon one of the leading newspapers in the city called on General McDermott to meet with COPS to resolve the tension that was growing daily in the city.

Feeling the pressure, McDermott contacted Archbishop Furey, the Roman Catholic Archbishop of the Diocese of San Antonio, through the then president of the Tesco Corporation, Mr. West. On October 29, 1976, Mr. West wrote to the Archbishop, offering to pay $10,000 for the entrance fee that was required for him to become a board member of the EDF. The Archbishop replied, "I must suppose that your offer is made in good faith, but the road to hell is paved with good intentions.... You have openly insulted our Mexican American brethren." He cc'd his reply to Mr. West to General McDermott and to the COPS leadership.

I had been meeting with the archbishop during this time to keep him informed of what was taking place. He maintained his loyalty to the parishes that belonged to COPS, even though the archdiocese lost a few major donors. The General's attempt to drive a wedge between the Church and COPS had backfired powerfully.

After refusing a city councilman's request to the EDF to meet with COPS, and after I refused to meet with a staff member of the EDF alone, and after the archbishop refused to join the EDF Board, General McDermott finally called Ms. Gallego to arrange a meeting with the COPS leadership.

COPS had traversed the first and most important issue—that of recognition; for without recognition there cannot be negotiations. The word recognition means "to know again." General McDermott and San Antonio's leading CEOs were about to get to know the leaders of the most powerful Mexican American organization in an entirely new way.

Both sides agreed to bring four leaders and a staff person. Additionally, both sides agreed the media would not be invited to the meeting and neither side would not talk with the media if the negotiations became ongoing. It was also agreed a neutral site would be chosen for the meeting. The site selected was a room in the downtown YMCA. At that first meeting and at meetings thereafter, COPS had at least 50 leaders outside of the YMCA so the negotiating team could brief the leaders as to what was taking place in real time.

The first negotiating session was awkward and tense. It was clear that General McDermott was angry and resented being there. He was especially leery of Fr. Benavides. Like many of the corporate and political leaders, McDermott simply did not know how to deal with Fr. Benavides. For one, he was unlike any other priest he had ever encountered. Fr. Al operated with a controlled anger that was difficult for an opponent to deal with. Second, he was whip smart and fast on his feet. And third, he had the support and admiration of the entire COPS organization.

From COPS' perspective, the purpose of the first meeting was to get a second meeting. I know that sounds strange, but it is often true that the first meeting is just to establish ground rules and goals for future meetings, assuming there will be some. To do this, COPS needed to try to lower the temperature that everyone brought into the room, what Saul Alinsky called "depolarizing." This meant that COPS had to allow General McDermott to vent, but without allowing him to disrespect Ms. Gallego, Fr. Benavides, or the organization. To do this, Ms. Gallego asked each person to introduce himself or herself by stating what their hopes were for the future of San Antonio.

Introductions allowed each participant to reveal a side of their humanity.

Each member of the COPS team led off by telling a short story about themselves and their hopes and dreams for their family and for the city. The EDF members followed suit. The introductions allowed each participant to reveal a side of their humanity. This worked to lower the temperature in the room. At the end of the one-hour meeting, a date and time was set for a second meeting, with the date, time, and agenda for the second meeting agreed upon by both sides. This second session would focus on COPS' two demands: a retraction of the Fantus Report for its negative characterizations of Mexican American people and a commitment to recruit companies to come to San Antonio that paid or would pay their employees at least $15.00 per hour. The COPS team briefed the leaders outside, answered the members' questions, and set a date and time for a further briefing and a strategy session for the second meeting with EDF.

At the planning meeting, the leaders agreed their first demand was non-negotiable, but they also knew we would need to be flexible with regard to the second demand. The main point is that the organization wanted the corporate community's historic efforts to maintain San Antonio as a low-wage city to end.

We approached the second meeting with great trepidation. Failure to move towards an agreement would embolden COPS' political and corporate enemies to cast COPS as the major impediment to recruiting new companies to the city. At the planning meeting, we worked on three or four versions of the wording for the hourly wage demand that would maintain our intent but would not be rigid. Since we neither knew how the EDF would react to our proposal nor what they would propose, we agreed we would call for a five minute caucus during the meeting as often as the leaders felt it was necessary.

Before and after the first meeting, COPS had kept its word about shunning the press. This was duly noted by General McDermott as the second session started, which did a lot to break the tension. In organizing, every step toward building trust is important. The second session would either result in progress toward an agreement or we would find ourselves in a long, protracted fight that could potentially bury us. What we did not fully account for was the EDF recognizing that they, too, needed an agreement. The band-aid of historical injustices had been torn off by COPS and was now bleeding publicly.

Ms. Gallego started the meeting by restructuring the organization's two demands. On the $15.00 per hour demand, she presented some alternative language, while the first <u>demand for an apology</u> remained the same. The EDF countered with very weak language on both points. After about fifteen minutes of back and forth that was going nowhere, Fr. Al called for a caucus. COPS stayed in the room as the EDF representatives retired to another room.

During the caucus, we were able to verbalize that we all sensed the EDF leaders were searching for a way to come to an agreement. While they had moved on language in regard to the first demand, their proposed language regarding the second demand (recruiting only companies that paid $15.00 an hour to their employees) was too general for it to have any meaning. After a further hour of heated negotiations, both sides agreed to a third meeting. COPS and EDF agreed to send proposed language on the second demand to each other prior to the third meeting taking place. At the next planning meeting, prior to the third negotiating session, the leaders were cautiously optimistic. In regard to the second demand, the leaders developed language that would call on the EDF to <u>set as a goal the recruitment of companies</u>

that paid its employees $15.00 per hour and agree to present regular, off-the-record reports to COPS on their efforts. The leadership also requested that if an agreement was reached, the announcement should be made in front of the entire organization at the St. Henry's Church parish hall, which was in the heart of one of the Mexican American neighborhoods. This agenda was sent in writing to the EDF.

The leaders entered the third negotiating session with anxiety and anticipation. Their anxiety was soon dissolved. Except for a few minor changes, the EDF accepted COPS' proposed language regarding both demands. COPS' final request to conduct a public signing ceremony at St. Henry's parish hall was countered by the EDF with a suggestion that we hold a joint press conference at noon at a downtown location. Fr. Al argued that their presence at St. Henry's would convey more meaning than they possibly could imagine. This time, the EDF team called for a caucus. When they returned, they agreed to COPS final request. The time and the date for the signing of the historic agreement was set. When the COPS team went outside to brief the group, some of whom had stood outside for all three negotiating sessions, the group started to chant "Viva COPS!"

On the night of May 30, 1977, at 6:00 pm, one hour before the action was to begin, the parish hall at St. Henry's was packed with over 1,000 COPS members. By 7:15, people were standing outside. The hall was very uncomfortable, as the evening was extremely hot and the hall had no air conditioning. The fans were just blowing hot air on everyone. At 7:30, Ms. Gallego, Fr. Benavides, and other COPS leaders were joined on the stage by General McDermott and two other EDF leaders.

General McDermott believed with the signing of this agreement San Antonio was ready for a new day.

I was able to get a note to Ms. Gallego to cut the time of the meeting in half due to the conditions in the hall. After saying a few words, Ms. Gallego invited General McDermott to address the membership. He remarked that COPS and the EDF had experienced some difficult times and negotiations, but that he believed with the signing of this agreement San Antonio was ready for a new day. The crowd gave him generous applause.

Then Ms. Gallego introduced Fr. Benavides. The crowd erupted. It took Fr. Al a good while to quiet the crowd. After giving a short, eloquent talk, he invited General McDermott to join him at the center of the stage to sign the agreement, a copy of which all present had in their hands.

After they signed the agreement, Fr. Benevides shook McDermott's hand and raised their clasped hands in the air like candidates at a political rally. The energy and emotion in the hall were electric. I felt as if I had been lifted out of my body. As I looked around the hall, I saw hundreds of people hugging, shouting, and crying. I had never experienced anything like it before. This scene continued for at least 15 minutes.

There was no way we would be able to conduct an evaluation at the end of this meeting, as is the IAF tradition. We all just let the joy soak in. I spent over an hour in the St. Henry's parking lot shaking hands and hugging members. When I finally began to drive home, one word came into my mind: "ecstasy." Entering my house, I went straight to the dictionary to look up that word. Here is the definition: 1) feeling or expressing overwhelming happiness or joyful excitement; euphoria, rapturous, overjoyed, blissful; 2) involving an experience of mystic self-transcendence.

Here is what Andy Sarabia wrote in his diary after the action, "San Antonio will no longer be known as a cheap labor town.... This event is historic in San Antonio.... The Mexican-Americans of San Antonio have brought Robert McDermott, Harold O'Kelly, and Ralph Thomas, representatives of the business sector, to St. Henry's Church in our community for this signing.... COPS has power! But never in my wildest dreams did I think I would witness an event such as this."

THREE

YOU PEOPLE

I n June of 1980, I moved to Baltimore City with my family to become the lead organizer of BUILD (Baltimorians United In Leadership Development). I had left the Industrial Areas Foundation (IAF) in 1978 to teach at San Jose State University School of Social Work, but after teaching organizing to undergraduate and graduate students, I became restless. I wanted to get back on the ground.

I met with Ed Chambers, the executive director of the Industrial Areas Foundation, to tell him that I wanted to return to the IAF. My one request was that I wanted to work with an organization on the east coast as both my wife's and my families lived there. Ed asked me to go to Baltimore. Baltimore was the first predominately African American city that the IAF had gone into since the late 1960s.

By 1980, BUILD, which the IAF founded in 1977, was in danger of collapsing. In fact, if Ed had not prevailed upon Mike Gecan to spend 75 percent of his time in Baltimore in the late 1970s to assist BUILD's leaders and staff, the organization would have surely died.

Mike, with whom I have partnered for forty years to build Metro IAF, a collective of over 20 organizations in eight states east of the Mississippi, is a phenomenal organizer. He has the anger, intelligence, imagination, and compassion that makes him the best organizer I have ever worked with.

Globalization and the financialization of the US economy had gutted Baltimore as a city where blue collar people once thrived. Another destructive force was racism. Maryland maintained segregated schools until the 1960s. To avoid allowing African Americans to attend the University of Maryland, the state paid the tuition fees for qualified minority students so that they would attend out of state colleges.

The port of Baltimore and the good paying, unskilled, and semi-skilled factory jobs that it generated had been a magnet for many European ethnic groups and for African Americans from the south. The city had a split and disconnected personality. On the one hand, it felt like a bustling northern city; on the other hand, it possessed the culture of a southern city in many ways. I soon became keenly aware of Baltimore's unhealthy social and political dynamics.

Baltimore had a split and disconnected personality.

When he had recruited me to take the job, Ed Chambers told me that although BUILD was floundering he had three reasons to believe in its possibilities. Their names were Monsignor Clare O'Dwyer, Rev. Wendell Phillips, and Rev. Vernon Dobson.

Unfortunately for me, when I began my work in September of 1980, Msgr. O'Dwyer had just announced his retirement. So much for the first leg of my BUILD leadership stool!

My first meeting with Rev. Phillips, on the other hand, was a total surprise. I did not know what to expect, since I had not met him during my interviews with the leaders in March 1980. When I called him for a one-to-one, he told me to meet him on the front porch of his home. As I sat waiting for him, I heard a loud roar from a huge motorcycle coming down the street. The man driving the bike pulled into the driveway next to the porch where I was sitting. He was a very large Black man with long hair, wearing a torn tee shirt and torn shorts. He got off his motorbike and yelled, "Are you Arnie Graf?" He came onto the porch, offered me a drink, and then began talking. I quickly realized what an intelligent, engaging, humorous man I was with. Rev. Phillips had striking blue eyes, a huge stomach, an infectious laugh, and an engaging mind. He had founded the first African American United Church of Christ congregation in Baltimore.

After asking me about my background and past experiences, he told me of his long engagement with the Black civil rights struggles in Baltimore. Later, as I got to know his congregation, I met some of his wonderful leaders. Some of them became part of the initial corps of leaders who reorganized BUILD. I often visited the pastor in his office, and on his desk was a big sign that said, "Baby Blue." I stopped by there for support, advice, laughter, and intellectual stimulation. He was a unique person who showed me a lot of love. Rev. Phillips had strong doubts about BUILD's viability, but he promised now that I was on the job he would take a wait and see approach rather than leave the organization.

My next visit was to the third leg of the stool, Rev. Vernon Dobson, the pastor of Union Baptist Church. In Rev. Dobson, I eventually found a mentor, pastor, teacher, colleague, and dear friend. His nickname in the community was "father," because people from all walks of life came to him for assistance and advice. The constant stream of people who came to his office ranged from addicts and homeless people to city council members, congresspeople, and senators. He was a lion of a man. His voice boomed. His anger and his humor were both dramatic and contagious—a unique combination. I instinctively knew I had to connect to Rev. Dobson in a special way as Msgr. O'Dwyer had retired and Rev. Phillips was, at best, very skeptical about BUILD's future.

As unusual as my first meeting with Rev. Phillips had been, however, elements of my first meeting with Rev. Dobson left me feeling confused and defeated. As I drove up to Union Baptist Church for my scheduled meeting with him, I saw a group of African American men arguing loudly. As I got out of my car, I observed Rev. Dobson in the middle of the group talking louder than anyone else. As I stood there taking in the scene, a white man in a pick-up truck parked behind me. The man got out of his truck and walked into the screaming group and at the top of his lungs yelled, "Is Shorty Red here?" The group got quiet and stared at the man.

Rev. Dobson yelled at the man, "What do you want with him?" The man said that he wanted to buy more of the bricks that Shorty was selling him for 25 cents per brick. Just at that moment, a short man with red hair took off down the street like a bat out of hell. After a couple of seconds, the entire group, with Rev. Dobson in the lead, took off after Shorty. Rev. Dobson was yelling, "Shorty, if I catch you, I am going to kill you!"

I soon learned that "Shorty Red" was one of the many people that Rev. Dobson looked after. It seemed that Shorty—instead of helping Rev. Dobson's crew build a coffee house on the corner of Dolphin and Lanvale as a place where people from the community could gather in a safe and comfortable place—was selling the bricks at night to this white guy for a quarter a brick!

And here I was, the new lead organizer of BUILD, an organization that had dwindled to only ten congregations and was $32,000 in debt, standing across the street from Union Baptist Church, watching the third leg of the stool running down the street threatening a man's life!

I got into my car and sat there feeling confused, lost and hopeless.

After a while, I started to drive aimlessly around the neighborhood. At some point I began to take in the scenery: hundreds of abandoned homes, trash strewn everywhere, broken glass-filled vacant lots, men standing on corners with vacant eyes, young women crossing the streets with baby carriages, children laughing and playing, police and ambulance sirens blasting constantly, elderly people sitting on their stoops talking with one another, and teenagers playing basketball in schoolyards—just as I had done growing up in New York City.

The next day, I arose ready to work—albeit unsure of what to do with such a weak organization in such a distressed city.

The second action was to embark on a two-month individual meeting campaign.

The first thing I did was to call John Moyer, an old friend from the National UCC Church, to ask him to send BUILD $10,000 so we could have a few months of breathing space. The second action I took was to embark on a two-month individual meeting campaign. To do this, I got the pastors of the one remaining congregations in BUILD to give me the names of the people who led their key congregational organizations.

The initial list was small but it soon grew as the leaders gave me more names. I was not seeking the names of "social justice leaders." Instead, I asked for the names of people who led the congregation's capital fund drive, and those that chaired their trustee boards and their deaconesses boards. I also asked for names of PTA presidents, neighborhood association leaders, and leaders of fraternities and sororities. I asked people who gave me names to call their friends to credential me so they would be willing to meet.

Over the next eight weeks, I met with over 250 people individually for 30-60 minutes each. The people I met lived all over the city. They were an economically diverse group: some middle-class, some working class, and some low income. Most were leaders or at least active in their church, school, or neighborhood in one way or the other. I met Vivian Washington, the woman who founded the Pacquin School, the first public high school for pregnant teenagers. I met successful doctors, lawyers, dentists and accountants. I met Wendell Wright, a lover of classical music who raised scholarship money for Black artists to pursue their careers. I met numerous teachers, principals, and adults who ran athletic and social clubs for youth and teenagers. I heard stirring choirs and powerful preaching. I met people who were true historians and storytellers.

I also met many struggling mothers and fathers who were too scarred to even want to believe that anything could change. While I saw some of the failings of the church, I also saw the strength, grace, power and beauty of the Black church. In my meetings, I was listening for three things. First, I was listening for people's personal stories; second, I tried to find out if they had a following; and, third, I wanted to find out if any of them had an appetite to act publicly on the issues of concern they raised.

After every individual meeting I had, I wrote a

brief summary on an index card highlighting a story that I heard, the problem areas that people raised, and a notation of other organizations they belonged to and if they were willing to act on the areas of their concern. I also noted the names of other leaders they suggested I meet with. While people raised education, youth concerns, crime, housing, and unemployment as issues of concern, underlying all of these issues were race and racism.

Underlying all of these issues were race and racism.

Deciding on an issue to attack that would result in a meaningful victory was a difficult task, given BUILD's lack of power at the time.

As I listened to people, however, the lack of affordable housing often came up. I knew from my previous organizing experience in Milwaukee that local banks often "red-lined" African American neighborhoods. Red-lining is the practice by banks of drawing red lines around neighborhoods where they would not make home mortgage or rehab loans. While no bank would admit to this practice, I knew that we could get the records of every bank's lending practices through the Community Reinvestment Act (CRA). This Act was passed by Congress in the 1970s—a victory that our organization in Milwaukee was tangentially involved in at the time. As I asked people who raised housing as an issue about the behavior of Baltimore's banks, many said that it was extremely difficult, if not impossible, to get a mortgage or home improvement loan in the neighborhood where they lived.

I began to agitate around the behavior of Baltimore's banks toward the Black community, and I discovered that the banks, with their big presence downtown, stood out as a symbol of the resentment that many people felt toward the white power establishment in the city. I received a visceral response from many leaders, especially when I told them that through the CRA we would be able to prove the banks' racist policies. While skeptical, a number of people volunteered to get the lending information on each bank and tabulate the data of mortgage loans by zip code for the year 1979. What we learned was that out of the $426 million in mortgage loans granted by all of the major banks in Baltimore that year, only 1.6% of those loans were made to the zip codes that represented the Black neighborhoods in the city. Given that 60% of Baltimore's population was African American, this statistic even astounded leaders like Rev. Dobson.

The first step BUILD needed to take was to organize as many people as possible to reveal our findings to a broad cross-section of people in as dramatic a way as possible. To do this, I met with the pastors and lay leaders that still belonged to BUILD. I also called all the people who had raised housing and racist bank behavior with me during my individual meetings. The leadership team and I asked people to come to Our Lady of Lourdes Roman Catholic Church to see the proof that we had uncovered. Additionally, we worked hard to get the media there.

We brought a couple of leaders from each member congregation to plan the agenda and to select the spokespeople. I taught that night that an action is like a three-act drama. Before the play, we needed to work on the logistics and do a rehearsal. We asked the leaders to pledge as to how many people they committed to bring to Our Lady of Lourdes on the night of the action. Our goal was to fill the basement of the church with 225 people. After two rehearsals, we were as ready as we were going to be.

I did not sleep much the night before the action. I knew that if this action was a failure, we would most likely have to end our effort in Baltimore. About 15 minutes before the action, the room was only half filled, but in the next 15 minutes the rest of the room filled up. In fact, we had to set up more chairs to accommodate everyone. Putting out additional chairs is an organizer's delight. The leaders and I were feeling good. Even the media showed up and, very importantly, Rev. Dobson and Rev. Phillips came.

We had great visuals that showed the mortgage lending practice by every bank in the year 1979 by zip code. Fr. Eugene J. McKenna, SSJ, a wonderful man, revealed the data for each bank in a very dramatic way. People booed spontaneously as the results of each bank were revealed. The action ended with volunteers signing up to meet with various bank presidents.

The next morning, I sat in the BUILD office reading the press accounts of our action—waiting to hear from some of the bank presidents' response to BUILD's request to meet with them. After waiting by the phone over two hours, I knew no bank president had any intention of reacting to BUILD's request to meet. (The first issue for this organization, as always, was recognition. Without recognition, you do not exist.) The leaders were simultaneously deeply disappointed and incensed by being ignored. They called an emergency meeting to decide on what to do next. I had met with the members of the planning team individually. Their responses ranged from, "I told you so" to a desire not to give up.

The leaders were deeply disappointed and incensed by being ignored.

At the next meeting, I began with a training session on the ingredients of power. Boiled down to their essence, they are organized people and organized money. I asked the leaders how much money they thought that their congregations, schools, Head Start Centers, and other institutions—as well as their individual members—had in a bank. At the next meeting, I took 45 minutes to teach that money was an important source of power. We dedicated the next 45 minutes to fleshing out a proposal: doing an anonymous survey in the member congregations to see where people and their congregations, organizations, and members banked and to ascertain how much money they had in their accounts.

Getting the congregations' budgets for their church, schools and other organizations was the easy part; finding out where and how much money people had in their accounts, even though the survey was to be anonymous, was going to be the hard part. To obtain the various pastors' agreement to this idea, we held a clergy meeting to get their buy-in. Additionally, the lay leaders met with their pastors to ask them to take the lead on this idea, because without the pastors' leadership, this idea would never take place. With the pastors' agreements, BUILD held Survey Sunday.

The leaders collected the surveys at the end of each Sunday service and then tabulated the results. To their surprise, the total that their members, congregations, and other people's institutions they controlled had sitting in the banks that refused to meet was $15 million. While objectively in a modern economy this is not a lot of money, it was certainly much more than the leaders had expected. The reality of controlling $15 million emboldened the leaders. The leaders next step was to call a meeting of the BUILD membership to review the results of the survey. This time there was no concern about the size of the turnout.

Phyllis Douglas, BUILD's president, and Fr. McKenna did an excellent job in walking through the results of the survey. To pour salt in the banks; wound, we had learned from Vinnie Quayle, the director of St. Ambrose Housing, a well-respected nonprofit affordable housing organization, that there was a Maryland State law that guaranteed mortgage loans made by banks under a certain amount of money to qualified borrowers. This meant that banks willing to make loans to mostly African American city residents would not lose any money even if the borrower defaulted on the mortgage payments. This fact, plus having $15 million in the banks, emboldened the people to act if the bank presidents continued to refuse to meet with BUILD.

After this internal money organizing action, which was covered by the media, two bank presidents called the BUILD office to schedule a meeting. The leaders decided on three demands. First, stop redlining their communities; second, match dollar for dollar in mortgage lending money to Black communities with the amount that the BUILD congregations had organized in each bank; and third, agree to hold quarterly meetings with the organization so that we could hold the banks accountable.

The first meeting was with a relatively small bank. While denying any practice of redlining, the president of the bank signed the agreement within 30 minutes. The leaders were ecstatic. "We won!"

The second bank that we met with was the largest savings and loan in Baltimore City. The leaders and I were not sure what to expect; however, the results were similar to the first bank's results. BUILD was on a roll. The leaders were beside themselves with joy, but I was beside myself with anxiety. This was way too easy. Perhaps we had not asked for enough. I was concerned that if every bank acted this readily the organization would not have been tested and the wrong lessons would have been learned. The leaders, I feared, would conclude that winning could come from clever research and minimal hard, public action. They would not have learned that it was going to take tension-filled actions to get

The leaders were beside themselves with joy, but I was beside myself with anxiety.

the entrenched political and corporate power players to create significant change.

The leaders wanted to meet with every bank president on our list. First, this would take forever, and we did not have "forever" money in the organization's bank account; second, even if every bank came to agreement, the victories would not significantly change the power dynamics that were at play in the city.

The leaders' desire to meet with every bank president was understandable. Why rock the boat? We were winning, and it sure felt good to finally get some respect. I realized two things. One, I could not convince the leaders to change their minds about meeting with every bank; and two, I could not think of anything else to propose that was doable in the short period of time that we had financially.

Here's what happened: the opposition, as it often does, organized our people for us. We had decided to meet with the bank president of Provident Savings

Bank, because Provident was large and had a number of local branches in the African American neighborhoods. BUILD needed to get Mr. Mason, the bank president, to react in a way that would reveal to the leaders what truly lay behind the façade of the accommodating, smiling faces of the two bank presidents that the leaders had met with. He obliged.

When we met with Mason, he had us escorted to a room in the basement of the bank. After a few minutes of having us wait, he arrived with an assistant. He proceeded to go around the table where we were seated shaking hands and welcoming each member of our delegation. When he sat down, each leader introduced himself or herself by saying a few words about themselves and the congregations where they belonged, as we usually do.

Mason listened politely, said a few words about himself and then, paying no attention to the agenda we had given him, zeroed in on Fr. Eugene McKenna. He told Fr. McKenna that his nephew was in the seminary studying to become a priest and of how proud he was of him. He showered Fr. McKenna with praise and admiration for dedicating his life to the priesthood and asked him to "keep an eye out" for his nephew. Fr. McKenna became wrapped up in the details of Mr. Mason's nephew's life. I was staring at the priest with eyes that said, "Please get down to business," but he was too enthralled in his conversation to notice me.

As I looked around the room, it seemed to me that everyone was enjoying Mr. Mason's conversation with Fr. McKenna far too much. Prior to this meeting, I had led a couple of workshops on the difference between "public" and "private" relationships. This workshop was part of the curriculum of universal principles that the IAF had developed over the years and taught at our national training sessions for leaders from around the country.

The essence of "Public and Private Life" training is for leaders to gain an understanding of the different things we seek and expect in our public and private relationships. For example, in our private relationships, while we obviously desire respect, wanting to be liked or even loved usually takes precedence; however, in our public relationships, while we want to be liked, respect is paramount. This is an easy concept to describe, but it is difficult to act on because the drive to be liked is very powerful.

The bank president was skillfully using the priest's natural desire to be liked by a fellow Catholic (especially one with a seminarian in the family) with his job as a spokesperson for BUILD to command respect as a leader of a powerful community organization. (Madison Avenue and many politicians are excellent at doing this.) If this line of conversation had persisted, the leaders would have left the meeting believing that Mr. Mason was a nice guy, but we would have accomplished nothing. I kept nudging BUILD's president, Ms. Douglas, to intervene, but she was too unsure of how to interrupt the lovefest that was taking place.

I knew I had to do something, but what? Since I could not think of anything else to do and calling for a caucus would only have created more confusion amongst the leaders, I took a risk. I began to bang on the table with my fist. The conversation between

Mr. Mason and Fr. McKenna came to an abrupt halt. Everyone's eyes turned towards me—thinking that I had lost my mind.

Mason turned to me and asked me what was wrong. I kept banging on the table trying to think of what to say. Finally, I looked him in the eye and said he was wasting our time. I said that the meeting was scheduled for only 45 minutes and we had just spent 15 minutes talking about his nephew the seminarian and not about red lining. I said, "Mr. Mason, what is your answer to our demands?" The leaders looked at me with confused anger, but they did not turn on me publicly.

Mason became upset. He said that he was showing complete respect for us, but I shot back that if he really respected us, he would answer our demands. I repeated our demands on the mortgages and said, "Yes or no!" The room filled with tension. I could see that Mason was trying to control his anger as he stared me down. He gathered himself and began to recite all the contributions the bank had made to various non-profits in the community. I cut him off and again demanded a yes or no answer.

At that point, Mr. Mason lost it. His next words saved the day…and perhaps the entire organization. "Do you know what is wrong with you people?" he snarled. "All you want is welfare. Why don't you people get a job!"

Now, here is the thing. In a Black community, the phrase "You People" is an only slightly less offensive way to say the n-word. Mason, by using the contemptible phrase, let the leaders of BUILD know what he really thought of them. He once again proved that it is your opponent's reaction that builds your power and allows you to win. Among them were three of the community leaders Mason talking to: Mr. Pervis Bates, a leader from Union Baptist Church, a retired colonel, who had fought in WWII, Korea, and Vietnam; Ms. Phyllis Douglas, a respected retired schoolteacher; and Fr. Eugene McKenna, one of the best Catholic pastors in the Archdiocese of Baltimore.

It is your opponent's reaction that builds your power and allows you to win.

The mood in the room shifted quickly. No one was smiling now. Ms. Douglas rose from her chair and told Mr. Mason that we did not have to "listen to this garbage." She looked at everyone and said, "We are leaving!" At that, everyone followed her out of the room.

We all went back to Union Baptist Church to evaluate what had just happened. Immediately after every action—no matter how big or small—in organizing, it is very important to conduct an evaluation. It is the only time you can get people who just had a common experience—but most likely have different interpretations of what they have just witnessed—to talk about how they feel, digest the lessons they may have learned, and talk about what they did right and what they could have done better. It is the single most effective way to do leadership training and development, much more effective than any reading or formal training session.

Evaluations are also the time for the leaders and organizers to measure whether or not they had reached the objectives we had set out to accomplish with the action we had just taken. If we did, why did it work? If we didn't, what went wrong? How did the leaders do? How did the organizer do? What, if anything, did we learn from our opponent's reaction to our demands? What organizing universals that we talk about so often did we experience? Finally, the evaluation allows the group to leave with a clear understanding of and commitment to the next step that needs to be taken.

In my experience, too often organizers and leaders fail to explore and the digest the organizing lessons they just experienced in real time. I learned this lesson the hard way. In 1971, I participated in an Industrial Areas Foundation training session in Chicago taught by the IAF founder, Saul Alinsky (who died unexpectedly the following year). His topic was "Action-Reaction." Alinsky asked volunteers to describe an action they had organized or participated in. After he called on a few of the new trainees, he called on me. I talked about demonstrations, pickets, sit-ins, going to jail, and so on. Alinsky seemed to be listening very intently to me, and I was feeling good as he egged me on. That is, until he cut me off and said, "Young man, you sound like a pile of undigested actions."

In that one sentence, Alinsky cut me down to size, but I learned a valuable lesson. What had I actually learned from all the frenetic action I had been involved in? I never forgot that lesson, and it is the reason I am so committed to the immediate-evaluation process.

At Union Baptist that day, we settled down and began our evaluation. We started by asking everyone to express their feelings in one word. Feelings are the place to start, because we don't just operate from our heads. We learn and grow by also listening to our hearts and our guts. The BUILD leaders that day expressed a wide range of emotions—including confusion, resentment, and anger (some of it aimed at me for pounding the table, some at Mr. Mason for calling us "you people").

After exploring peoples' feelings about what actually happened at the meeting, I taught two political universals. The first was the connection between action, tension, and reaction. The second was the nature and meaning of public and private relationships. We then discussed what BUILD's next step should be. It was now clear to everyone that the large banks did not intend to change. We would have to engage them in a serious struggle if we were to accomplish meaningful results. We left setting a date and time for our next meeting. We closed out with prayer, as we always did—asking God for guidance and courage. It was one of the best evaluations we ever had. People understood what I had done and why I had done it.

It was clear to everyone that the large banks did not intend to change.

By the time we gathered again, I had met individually with everyone on the banking issue team. Most everyone wanted to take a next step but were unsure of what step that should be. During the individual meetings with each leader, I raised the idea of tying up Provident Bank's daily operation by having one-hundred BUILD members line up at each teller window to exchange one dollar for 100 pennies. I suggested that we continue this until Mr. Mason agreed to negotiate with us in good faith on our demands.

Some leaders loved the idea and some leaders were against it out of fear that we would all be arrested. I asked everyone to think about my idea and about any other tactics they thought might work in getting the bank's recognition and respect. I met with both Rev. Dobson and Rev. Phillips about my idea, and my suggestion of taking direct action at a major bank in downtown Baltimore is what began to gain Rev. Dobson's respect.

Colonel Bates, one of Rev. Dobson's deacons, who had been at the meeting, told Rev. Dobson that Mr. Mason had referred to us as "You People." The deacon's anger inspired Rev. Dobson, because

Mr. Bates was a conservative man in manner and in outlook. In fact, he had never been part of anything related to social action before he joined the negotiating team that had met with Mr. Mason.

Rev. Dobson loved the Black church with all of his heart. He was a friend of Dr. Martin Luther King, Jr., and whenever Dr. King or his aides came to Baltimore, they connected with Rev. Dobson. The thought that BUILD might become an organization through which the Black church would take on racism and injustice was what he had hoped for when Ed Chambers initially approached him. He was finally on board.

Everyone in the Black community seemed to know Rev. Dobson. It didn't matter if we were downtown or uptown, every Black person knew him and wanted to shake his hand. Eventually he took me under his wing, teaching me about the history and culture of the African American church. He gave me books to read by Howard Thurman, Henry Mitchell, and others. He sent me to various Sunday Services—some Baptist, some A.M.E., some evangelical—so that I could experience the wide range of the Black worship experience. He also taught me about Baltimore politics. He set up meetings with historians as well as retired activists and politicians for me to meet with.

I asked Rev. Dobson to come to the next leaders' meeting where we were going to consider tying up Provident Bank. I knew that if he came to the meeting, the anxiety level of the other leaders would decrease. Sure enough, when the leaders met, they were pleased to see Rev. Dobson and he was excellent during the discussion of the possible action on Provident Bank. He did not say a word until everyone had spoken. Most people liked the idea, but they were concerned about the police overreacting. Too many of the leaders had had bad experiences with "cowboy" police behavior in Baltimore.

After a long discussion of the pros and cons of the proposed action, Rev. Dobson spoke. He said that the action was necessary. He assured people that there would be no violence or arrests because everything we would be doing was completely legal. He said that we would be disciplined. He also promised that we would have fun!

The leaders voted to go forward. At the final rehearsal, Rev. Dobson and Rev. Phillips kept everyone loose and laughing. BUILD was ready. The next day, we had two buses to bring people to the bank. Two bus captains briefed people one more time on our way to the bank.

We chose a Friday at 11:30 am to gather at the downtown branch, both because Mason had his office there and because it was at this time that Provident customers who worked downtown cashed their paychecks over their lunch hour before returning to work. By noon, when the bank's customers began to arrive, they had to go to the end of the lines behind our 100 people. We hoped that customer patience would wear thin.

After our evening rehearsal the night before the action, Rev. Dobson had pulled me to the side to tell me to expect a large police contingent and canine units to be at the bank to greet us that next morning. I was skeptical of this because I had done this action in Chicago and Milwaukee and had never encountered police dogs. Although I thought he was being overly dramatic, I took his advice to have a pastor, wearing a collar, stand in between every twenty people in line. He also said that he would handle the police and the canine units. As the buses pulled up to let us off, I quickly realized that Rev. Dobson was right. There were at least 12 cops, two paddy wagons, and two canine units stationed in front of the bank.

As the buses pulled up to let us off, the dogs were barking loudly as their handlers strained to hold them back. I could feel my tension, as well as everyone else's tension, as we disembarked. Some people instinctively began to sing as we lined up in front of the bank. This seemed to lift the anxiety everyone was experiencing. At 12:00, the first twenty people, including me, Ms. Douglas, Rev. Phillips. and a few other pastors entered the bank. Rev. Dobson stayed outside to deal with the police and to keep the people in the line calm.

One of the pastors who was with the first group to enter the bank was Rev. Douglas Miles. Rev. Dobson had sent me to meet him a couple of months before this action. Rev. Miles was very reluctant to meet with me; however, after he stood me up a few times (mostly, I think, to see if I was persistent), we finally met in his office.

Rev. Miles was a young pastor at the time who I quickly learned displayed extraordinary political acumen for someone his age. He had been born and raised in Baltimore City. After he graduated from Douglas High School in Baltimore, Rev. Miles went to Johns Hopkins University. He told me about boarding the bus in his all-Black neighborhood to go to Hopkins. When he boarded the bus, all the passengers were Black. By the time the bus reached Johns Hopkins, he was the only African American on the bus. Upon graduating from Johns Hopkins, he had taken a job as a local bank manager. After a couple of years in this position, he and his wife applied for a home mortgage loan. Even though he worked for the bank and qualified for the loan, he was turned down. Soon after this experience, he left the bank and responded to a call to ministry. He became the pastor of Brown Memorial Baptist Church, a small church on the city's west side Black community. In a few years, under his leadership, the church grew to 1500 members and moved to a much larger facility.

Most of Rev. Miles' social action took place under the auspices of the Baptist Ministers Conference and the Interdenominational Ministers Alliance. At one point, he joined some of the ministers from the Baptist Ministers Conference to meet with Alan Hoblitzell, the president of Maryland National Bank. At the time, Maryland National Bank was the largest bank in Maryland. When Rev. Miles arrived at the bank for the meeting, instead of 30 pastors that had committed to be there, there were only a handful of clergy present.

Mr. Hoblitzell, who years later became an ally of BUILD (but only after a long and contentious fight with the organization), ushered the clergy into a basement meeting room. There, he lectured the pastors on what the bank would and would not do. After Mr. Hoblitzell's short, humiliating lecture, the clergy were ushered out of the bank. Rev. Miles told me that he felt as if he had been kicked in the stomach. He and the pastors felt humiliated and powerless. From that point on, as much as Rev. Miles respected Rev. Dobson, he vowed to never again get involved in social action.

As we talked, I told him of BUILD's plans to disrupt Provident Bank's business until we finalized an agreement to end Provident's racist red-lining practices. I promised him that there would be 100 people at the action and that we would be disciplined. When I saw Rev. Miles in line in front of the bank, I was ecstatic. I knew that he was young, talented, angry, and charismatic. I hoped that BUILD's action would capture his anger and imagination.

As the first 20 BUILD members lined up at the teller windows, the lead security guard approached the BUILD members lined up at the teller windows. Ms. Douglas, Rev. Miles, a few other leaders, and I intercepted him as he approached. Ms. Douglas asked him what the problem was, and he shouted at her that we all had to leave the bank immediately. Ms. Douglas told him calmly that we were there to do business. The guard became incensed. He went outside to bring in the police to arrest us. As the police came into the bank, the media followed them. The security guard, now totally out of control, pushed a TV cameraman into the revolving front door. The cameraman cut his eye, and that upset the media. They came pouring into the bank to film everything that was going on.

Outside, the bank's normal customers were in fact becoming impatient as they needed to cash their paychecks and return to work. As far as I was concerned, I knew that Rev. Dobson had everything under control outside. In fact, as I stepped outside, I could hear everyone in line singing at the top of their lungs. Inside the bank, the security guard ordered the police to arrest us. The leaders continued to stand in line exchanging dollars for pennies.

We were in a faceoff when the security guard heard the police sergeant's commander at headquarters ask him over his walkie talkie; "What is going on there?!!" He reminded the sergeant that he had 12 officers, two canine units, and two paddy wagons tied up at the bank. The sergeant looked befuddled. The security guard was yelling at him, "Arrest them, arrest them!" The sergeant asked, "On what charge?" The security guard shot back, "For making change!" Immediately the commander yelled over the walkie talkie, "You can't arrest people for asking for change in a bank!" He ordered all the police to leave the bank and return to headquarters.

Our team was trying unsuccessfully to keep straight faces. The scene looked and felt like something out of a bad TV sitcom. When the police left the bank, the media surrounded our team and the security guard. At that point, the security guard asked Ms. Douglas what it would take for us to leave the bank. She told him that we would leave after he escorted us upstairs to meet Mr. Mason to schedule a meeting with the bank president within one week. People were standing tall and proud as the security guard went upstairs.

After a few minutes, we were all escorted upstairs to the executive office. The meeting that BUILD proposed had only two demands. First, would the bank make $4.2M in mortgage loans in BUILD's neighborhoods—the amount of money that BUILD churches and members had on deposit at Provident Bank? And would the bank meet quarterly with BUILD to verify that loans were in fact being made?

The day's victory belonged to everyone assembled. The BUILD leadership team of four were ushered in to Mr. Mason's office. He was angry but restrained. Ms. Douglas told him we wanted to schedule a meeting with him to negotiate our demands within two weeks. The bank president took the team into his appointment secretary's office to set up a date and time to meet with us.

On the way downstairs, we could hardly contain ourselves. We caucused briefly before going outside, where the rest of our members had gathered. The media were all assembled. Ms. Douglas announced the good news. She then said that the day's victory belonged to everyone assembled. She concluded her brief remarks by telling everyone that it was BUILD's hope that the bank would negotiate in good faith, but if they did not we could expect to be returning to the bank! She then invited everyone to return to Union Baptist for refreshments and an evaluation.

When we arrived at Union Baptist, everyone was tired but looked as if they had just finished a delicious meal. As we ate, everyone told great stories about what they had experienced at the bank. At the end of the meal and the evaluation, Ms. Douglas took quotas for BUILD's next internal meeting. This meeting would be one of either celebration if they were successful in their negotiations with Provident Bank or decision on the next step to take if Mr. Mason failed to agree with the organization's demands. The commitments added up to 500 people. I was smiling from ear to ear as I listened to leaders taking these quotas, because just a few months earlier, we struggled to get six people willing to do some basic research on redlining.

Two weeks later, we met with Mr. Mason in the bank's main conference room. BUILD had ten leaders in the conference room and 50 leaders outside of the bank. Mason met us at the front door of the bank and escorted us into the conference room. He could not have been more respectful, and there was no mention of his seminarian nephew. Ms. Douglas told him that BUILD hoped that we could get past the last few contentious weeks to forge a relationship of mutual trust. Mason echoed the BUILD's president's words and quickly agreed to our two demands. The two signed the agreement that the organization had prepared and sent to him prior to the meeting. After shaking hands, Ms. Douglas led the entire delegation outside and held up the agreement for everyone to see, including the media.

Almost six months to the day, BUILD had gone from being an organization on life support to one that had grown from ten institutions to seventeen institutions and won new-found recognition in the city. Now, more than forty years after its founding, BUILD has grown into a persistent, powerful force in Baltimore City. The organization conceived of and forced the passage of the first Living Wage Ordinance in the country in 1994. This effort, which required over one year of public action and negotiation with the mayor and the city council to see passed, was soon followed by Metro IAF's successful campaign in New York City to pressure its mayor and city council to pass the second Living Wage Law in the United States.

Additionally, BUILD along with its partners has built over 1,000 affordable houses. Nearly 20 years ago it founded Child First—the largest after-school program in the city. It also brought to fruition "College Bound," a program has enabled thousands of Baltimore City public school students to attend college. Recently, it launched "Turn-Around-Tuesday," which over the last few years has trained and placed over 800 unemployed or formerly incarcerated people into good paying jobs. For the year 2018, the retention rate of the program was 81%.

Just as importantly, BUILD has trained and developed some of the finest leaders I ever worked with. From its struggling beginning over 40 years ago, here is how a *Baltimore Sun* recognized BUILD's successful negotiation with Under Armour, a powerful corporation, who agreed on a plan that included major commitments from the company in return for city subsidy for its massive $500 million development project: "The deal, which is unprecedented, significantly increases BUILD's clout as an organization that can negotiate in good faith and achieve results."

Amen.

FOUR

THE COLONY
ON THE MAINLAND

About ten minutes before the founding meeting of Washington Interfaith Network (WIN) was to take place, I took my seat on the stage of the historic Metropolitan A.M.E. Church and looked out over a crowd of eighteen hundred people seated in the sanctuary. I knew that there were an additional three hundred people watching on a large TV screen in the church's meeting hall. On one night, in one church, 2100 residents from every ward in the District of Columbia, a city of 700,000 in the nation's capitol, were waiting for an important event to begin. I was both exhilarated and exhausted by the beautiful sea of faces—exhausted, I assumed incorrectly, as a result of my hectic travel schedule and the preparations for this night.

Through that May 28, 1996, founding meeting,

I had felt as if I had dead weights in my shoes. Each day presented a challenge to stay sharp, alert, and upbeat. What I did not know was that I was dealing with prostate cancer. (I was extremely fortunate to have the cancerous prostate removed a few weeks later without having the cancer spread.)

To my left and to my right sat First Lady Hillary Clinton, HUD Secretary Henry Cisneros, District of Columbia Mayor Marion Barry, the President of Georgetown University, Fr. Leo J. Donovan, SJ, and a large number of WIN leaders. Behind us was the magnificent choir of St. Augustine's Roman Catholic Church —75 strong.

While the sounds and the sights of the event were powerful, what could not be seen in the room (except for their obvious fruits) were the thousands of individual meetings, hundreds of small house meetings, scores of training sessions, numerous research actions, and the process of identifying and developing a talented, powerful core of leaders who refused to be divided or distracted over the course of 1400 other nights that led up to this evening.

Washington, DC, is the home of national associations, powerful lobbyists, and thousands of political and ideological wannabees, but it is also the home of the kind of hard-working people who form the backbone of any American community.

When it comes to governance, DC is anything but normal. While the mayor and the city council have a number of assigned powers, Congress has the ultimate say over the city's budget and laws. Washington, DC, is the only "colony" left on America's mainland.

DC is divided geographically by Rock Creek Park and the Anacostia River. When I began organizing in 1992, west of the park was predominately populated by middle class and wealthy white residents, and east of the river was predominately populated by working and low-income African American residents. Most of the time the twain never met.

The fact that DC residents do not fully control their own destiny, and the fact that a persistent racial divide was ever present, made the idea of organizing a city-wide multiracial organization difficult to contemplate. Many attempts prior to this one had foundered.

I was struck by the hypocrisy of a nation that saw itself as a beacon of democracy but then allowed itself to be governed from a racially divided colony. But I was not naïve. I knew that to have a chance at success I would have to assemble a team of leaders who would be able and willing to live in the tension between urgency and patience—urgency about the depth and breadth of the challenge, and patience about what it would take to build enough power to challenge the "accepted" reality of DC's local politics and racial divide.

I would have to assemble a team of leaders willing to live in the tension between urgency and patience.

I was fortunate that in 1991 Doctor Lawrence Jones, Dean of the School of Religion at Howard University, had asked me to teach a course that I titled

"The Congregation as a Base for Social Change." I was honored to be asked to do this by Dean Jones because of the great respect I had for him. While teaching at Howard, I met many divinity students who were also working as part-time or full-time ministers at DC churches.

Some of these ministers had heard of the successes of the Industrial Areas Foundation (IAF) organizations in Baltimore and Brooklyn. With my help, two of them, Rev. William Bennett and Rev. Joseph Daniels, began to do a number of individual meetings with African American pastors throughout the District. The one thing I was certain of from the start, was that any effort in DC had to begin with the Black church. One of the pastors we met early on was Rev. Al Galman, pastor of Mt. Carmel Baptist Church. Rev. Galman took a lead role in calling together small groups of Black pastors at his church for me to meet with. Through Rev. Galman and Revs. Bennett and Daniels, I met a number of very talented pastors, including Rev. Lionel Edmonds, Pastor of Mt. Lebanon Baptist Church, and Rev. Darrell

Macklin, Pastor of St. Paul's Baptist Church. While different in style and background, both men were talented, engaging, and committed to a meaningful ministry in the city.

When I proposed to Ed Chambers, the executive director of the IAF at the time, that I wanted to organize in DC, he was one hundred percent against the idea. He pointed out that besides the fact that I was already overextended, there was no way that a local DC organization could hold a racist congressional committee, empowered to rule over the district, accountable. Objectively, I knew that he was correct on both counts, but after having met some of the clergy in DC, I knew I wanted to work with them to see if we could figure out a way forward. Once Ed agreed not to stand in my way, I went full steam ahead. The question in my mind was whether or not these clergy leaders would have the patience to take two to three years to build a power organization in the IAF tradition.

While racial division and animus are difficult to overcome everywhere in our country, it was particu-

larly acute at this time in DC. Mayor Marion Barry, as astute a politician as I had ever encountered,
was in some quarters of the city a symbol of Black
empowerment, while in other
quarters he was seen as a rogue,
an unscrupulous and divisive figure. He was actually both. Mayor
Barry was a unique character,
both uniquely talented and pro-
foundly flawed.

**Racism
and racial
tensions and
insecurities
permeated
every
institution,
every
controversy,
every
encounter.**

While I knew from previous
IAF experiences in cities like Baltimore, Memphis, Atlanta, Char-
lotte, and Milwaukee, that after
about an initial year of organizing
there would be both known and
unknown challenges, in the case
of DC, it was the racism and racial tensions and insecurities that permeated every institution, every controversy, and every encounter, including the building
of an institutionally based, multi-faith organization,
that made organizing especially difficult.

I had long ago learned that in each new place I worked as a white organizer, I would need to prove myself all over again. I also knew that being a Jewish person working with Christian and Muslim religious institutions always added some additional skepticism I would have to overcome.

In DC, in the early 1990s, other challenges—a severe income divide, poor police community relations, inadequate housing, poor-performing schools, and many of the other ills of all low-income communities—became glaringly evident within the first year of my work. In doing hundreds of individual meetings, I began to get an initial understanding of the alliances and factions that were present in the religious institutions and well-defined neighborhoods, as well as the role that the various corporations and their organizations played. Additionally, since so much of the land in the District is filled with non-profit, tax-exempt institutions and associations, I could see why the city struggled to generate enough revenue to provide for the needs of its residents.

LESSONS LEARNED

⤳

I spent at least seventy-five percent of my time in the first six months meeting individually and in small groups with African American pastors and their lay leaders. After six months, with the leadership of Revs. Bennett, Galman, Daniels, Edmonds, and Macklin, we convened thirty-five African American pastors to see if they would be willing to give me permission to initiate meetings with white clergy. It was essential that the invite to meet with white clergy come from them, and they agreed. As I met with many white clergy over the following months, I would reconvene the Black clergy to tell them what I learned. The white clergy basically fell into three categories. There were those who wanted nothing to do with this idea. (In one way or another, they claimed to have had bad experiences when they had dealt with African American clergy. One pastor told me he would have to be a masochist to sit through another meeting where he and his white privilege were identified as the cause of slavery and racism.) Other clergy expressed some interest in the idea of organizing, but were very skeptical about the possibilities of success. But a fair number of white pastors were very enthused about exploring the possibilities of building an organization across racial, economic, and geographic boundaries.

After about a year, the Black clergy voted to have me invite interested white clergy to a luncheon meeting. We met at a Black church, and after lunch those in attendance did twenty minutes of one-to-one relational meetings across racial lines. After the individual meetings, we had a rich group conversation about what people had learned from one another. We ended the meeting with an agreement to meet monthly, and each clergy person pledged to do at least three individual meetings with clergy they knew or would work to get to know. For the next six months, each clergy meeting began with individual meetings, and then I conducted 30-45-minute training sessions on the elements of building a broad based, diverse, city-wide organization.

During this process, some clergy dropped out, and some new clergy came on board. After about eighteen months, we had a core of about thirty-five clergy, some African American and some white, that began to gel. It was now time for the clergy to call together five to ten of their leading lay leaders to meet and hear from them what they had been doing and planning. The clergy chose to hold this initial meeting at Gethsemane Baptist Church. We expected about three hundred people to be at the meeting, and the challenge at the end of the meeting would be to see if we could get commitments from at least two hundred and fifty lay leaders to attend a series of three training sessions over the course of three weeks on the elements of building a broad-based organization.

We lined up various lay leaders to speak on some issues that the clergy believed we all had in common, and we selected a clergy leader to speak to the need for the creation of a racially diverse, broadly based, citywide organization. The clergy chose a Black pastor for the pivotal role of speaking to the role of race in the city and our need to recognize both the past and the present racial divide; however, he would also lay out the need to begin to write a new chapter in DC's life by forming a new organization

The agenda addressed some of the "knowns" that were present, e.g., poor schools, poverty, affordable housing. Fifteen minutes before the start of the meeting, we had over three hundred people seated, and we wound up with an overflow crowd. That's when I knew we had something real.

The first set of speakers did well, and the crowd was engaged and upbeat. Then the pastor whose talk was focused on the city's racial divide stood at the podium to speak. If he had stuck to his outline, I thought his talk would be honest, forthright, and hopeful. However, the "unknown" soon took place. As the pastor got into his talk, he veered unexpectedly into a mini-diatribe about a Roman Catholic parish in his congregation's neighborhood that he accused of being racist. The energy in the room went from hopeful to quiet unease. Those of us in the front looked at each other with disbelief and frustration. His diatribe lasted eight minutes, but it felt like an hour. I huddled with one of the Black pastors who was co-chairing the meeting and asked him to clean this up without embarrassing the speaker. Fortunately, the chair did a good job of getting us back on track and the meeting ended with the congregations in attendance committing to bring together two hundred and fifty lay leaders for the scheduled three-week training sessions.

The pastor who went off script did not stay for the evaluation after the meeting. When he and I met a few weeks after this meeting, he was somewhat defensive but also felt badly. He said that he intellectually agreed with what we were trying to do but realized he personally was not ready for this kind of effort. He and I agreed to meet periodically so I could keep him abreast of what was taking place. Three years later, his congregation joined the organization.

As we began to prepare for the three-week training sessions, a huge "unknown" exploded that left all of us wondering if our entire effort was doomed to an abrupt end. Due to the District's very poor financial situation, Congress announced that it was placing DC under the authority of a five-member congressionally appointed Financial Control Board. This newly appointed board was now completely in charge of DC's finances and budget! The Board was charged by Congress to stay in power until the members deemed the city's finances to be in good shape. The mayor and city council had now been completely emasculated. None of us had seen this coming. If this Board had been in place in 1992, I would never have started the journey. Now there was no one we could hold accountable—not even a constitutionally weak mayor and city council.

There was no one we could hold accountable— not even a constitutionally weak mayor and city council.

Between the announcement of the Control Board and the next scheduled clergy meeting, I met with each active clergy person. The leaders' responses were varied and scattered. Some said we should suspend our effort and others insisted we should forge ahead even though it was a mystery to all of us how we would do so effectively.

As I described in earlier chapters, there have been a number of times in my career that I have experienced an emotional meltdown. As in San Antonio, I again questioned myself deeply and harshly. Had I let my emotions take over clear thinking? Why had I not listened to Ed Chambers' advice? Had I led people into an unwinnable place? Once again, I experienced many sleepless nights.

Besides meeting with the active clergy, I decided to spend extended time with Rev. Edmonds, Macklin, and Daniels. I had a great deal of respect for each of these Black pastors, who were young, innovative risk takers and totally committed to the organizing process.

In particular, I became very close to Rev. Lionel Edmonds. His interests were wide and varied. He was as comfortable in the streets as Rev. Vernon Dobson had been when I first met him in Baltimore. Once Rev. Edmonds decided he could trust me, he became as determined and reliable a leader as I have ever worked with. Eventually, we became very good friends. If for no other reason, I did not want to give up on DC because I did not want to lose my relationship with these three men.

Each of these pastors in their own unique ways argued for us to stay the course. Essentially, they said that we had come too far by hard work and faith to quit now. They said that quitting now would mean it would take at least ten years to start another effort. I knew that they were right about that.

At the next clergy meeting, we presented three options: 1) end our effort; 2) suspend our effort and continue our clergy meetings so the relationships that had formed could stay alive; 3) keep going with the organizing effort despite this significant obstacle.

In addition to recognition, one of the many universals of all effective organizing is *ownership*. The organizer has to be sure to balance the drive to move forward with a healthy dose of *disinterest*—making sure that the ownership for forward motion is deeply felt and affirmed by the leaders involved.

After breaking into small groups to discuss these

options, the clergy reconvened and voted to plow ahead. This meant that our next step was to go as a group to a Control Board meeting. We decided we needed to run an action on the Control Board even before the first scheduled training sessions with the lay leaders.

On the day of our first action with the DC Control Board, twenty Washington Interfaith Network (WIN) clergy filled the few seats that were made available for the public. Three of them even took seats at the meeting table itself. WIN had written to the staff that the organization would be present and requested five minutes on the agenda to speak. The five members of the Control Board had been copied on our request.

When the members of the Control Board entered the meeting room, they seem startled. The chairman of the Control Board was Dr. Andrew Brimmer. Dr. Brimmer was a very bright and accomplished man. He was a noted economist, educator, and business leader. He was the first African American to have served as an appointed governor of the Federal Reserve System. He was also a very stiff and formal man and did not countenance any break in protocol. When he took his seat, he acknowledged our presence and informed us that we would have five minutes to speak at the end of the meeting. We had anticipated this and decided ahead of time to accept. At the end of the meeting, Dr. Brimmer called on WIN to take the five minutes we had requested. The WIN spokesperson took five minutes to request twenty minutes on the next agenda so that the fledgling organization could flesh out what a meaningful relationship would look like. Dr. Brimmer responded sternly and in no uncertain terms that we would not be allowed to speak at the next meeting or at any other meeting. We left the room telling Dr. Brimmer that we would see him at the next meeting.

The main purpose of the second meeting was to gain recognition from the Control Board so that we could negotiate with them. We knew that recognition, as always, was the essential first step.

At the WIN planning meeting before the second Control Board meeting, we role played as many different scenarios as we could imagine. What if security would not allow us access to the meeting room? What if we got in the room, but Dr. Brimmer had security try to remove us? What if Dr. Brimmer moved the meeting to another room in the building? And so on and so on.

We decided to disrupt the meeting at the beginning if we did not see WIN's issue at the beginning of the agenda. As we walked into the room about ten minutes early and did not see WIN on the agenda, Rev. Joe Daniels unexpectedly sat in Dr. Brimmer's seat. Like everyone else, I had no idea why he did this. I sat and pondered his action. However, I decided not to say anything to him. It was, as they say, a stroke of genius.

When the Board members entered the room, Dr. Brimmer stood behind Rev. Daniels and said, "You are in my seat!" The minister just looked forward and said nothing. I was anxious and not sure how this would play out. We had decided to disrupt the meeting, but not in this way. Rev. Daniels is a strikingly tall former college basketball player who is a strong, passionate, and engaging human being. As we watched this encounter unfold, I decided to trust his instinct and let the scene play itself out. Dr. Brimmer was beside himself. He was clearly offended and angry but not sure of what to do. Shortly, he summoned the security guards. When they entered the room, they looked befuddled. The room was quiet and everyone except Dr. Brimmer was seated and quiet. The officers were not sure what to do. Dr. Brimmer then yelled out as he pointed toward Rev. Daniels: "This man is in my seat!" It was apparent that some other board members were becoming uneasy with what was transpiring. They did not want to be part of physically removing twenty well-behaved and respected ministers from their seats, but they could see that Dr. Brimmer was nearly

I decided to trust Rev. Daniels' instinct and let the scene play itself out.

at the end of his patience.

It appeared that everyone was frozen in time. I then leaned over to two of the leaders and asked if I could speak. I sensed I had to break the stalemate before things got out of hand. When the leaders nodded OK to me, I got up and addressed Dr. Brimmer and the board members. I said that it was obvious how serious we were about being heard. I asked that they direct the chief of staff to meet with the leaders of WIN before the next Control Board meeting so that we could work out a mutually respectful way to work together before the next meeting took place.

I said that, for better or for worse, they were now our unelected representatives and that we had every intention of being involved in our future.

Perhaps to break the tension that appeared to be leading to a politically ugly scene, a couple of the board members spoke in favor of approving a meeting with the board's chief of staff. I then turned to the clergy and asked them if this idea was acceptable to them. When the clergy unanimously voted yes, I asked the Board if they were in agreement. When a

majority of the different members of the board nodded their heads yes, WIN leaders led our delegation
out of the room, leaving Dr. Brimmer standing next
to his seat, never having agreed to anything.

Our immediate evaluation of this action was both rich
and befuddling. We had run an action to get recognition. We seemed to have accomplished that; however,
much of what took place was totally unplanned. The
question on everyone's mind was directed to Rev.
Daniels. "Why did you sit in Dr. Brimmer's seat?" He
said he had done so instinctively. He said he knew
we planned to disrupt the meeting if we did not see
WIN on the agenda, which we did not, and when he
took Dr. Brimmer's seat and no one said anything, he
simply stayed there. He told us that he knew from
observing Dr. Brimmer in the first meeting that taking his seat of power might cause him to react.

We had accomplished what we had set out to do
and Rev. Daniels' action, even if unplanned, proved to

be a brilliant idea. I drove home feeling grateful that we had not given up when the Control Board had taken over the city. What Rev. Daniels did was terrific. WIN had a core of leaders who were not about to me intimidated, and I was very proud to be a part of this team.

Some years later, over lunch, I asked Joe Daniels to reflect upon his actions that day at the Control Board meeting. In his response, he reminded me of a small research action in the early days of organizing WIN. We had conducted a meeting with Dr. Stephen Trachtenburg, then President of George Washington University. While I remembered the meeting because Dr. Trachtenburg had been so arrogant, I did not remember that Joe had been part of that team. During the meeting, Trachtenburg had became increasingly agitated by our asking him how the university justified paying no taxes to the city given the multiple services the city provided to the university. After losing his patience with us, he had stood up and said, "This meeting is over."

Joe remembered leading our team out of the

university president's office with our heads hanging low. He recalled that he and I had walked to our cars together that day and I had agitated him about why he left Trachtenburg's office without protest. He told me he had felt there was no alternative at the time but that I had admonished him: "Never relinquish your seat at a power table until you and your team are ready to do so."

Joe Daniels vowed never to leave a seat at the table simply on the demand of a power person.

Rev. Daniels then said that after that lesson he had vowed never to leave a seat at a nego-tiating table simply upon the demand of a power person. So when Dr. Brimmer told him to get out of his seat at the Control Board meeting, he had simply kept his vow!

Before the meeting with the DC Control Board's chief of staff that had been "approved" at our action, Rev. Darrell Macklin called me up. He said that the Control Board had just offered him a job! Though Rev. Macklin has a quiet demeanor, he is a very strong person. His career, prior to being called to the ministry, was as a highly regarded computer analyst.

Dividing the opposition by offering one of the leaders a lucrative job or gift is a common tactic used by people with power; however, the Control Board did not understand what WIN's leading pastors were made of. Rev. Macklin told me that it took him less than one minute to reject their offer. The only thing that excited him about the offer was that he knew that we "had" them.

Recently, I asked Rev. Macklin to reflect on his experience with the Control Board. He said, "We did not realize it then, but this was our opportunity to build our organization from the bottom up. The Control Board took over from Mayor Barry, but in doing so, they gave us the opportunity to fill the vacuum that had been created."

When I spoke with Rev. Lionel Edmonds about the same series of actions with the Control Board, he told me they "gave WIN our chops." The actions took away any impression our leaders might have had of Washington business leaders as "big" people. "These actions with the Control Board gave us our identity," Rev. Edmonds pointed out.

One of the lessons I have learned from the IAF is that "the action is in the reaction." In this case, a seemingly insurmountable negative had turned into an enormous positive.

With a schedule of negotiating sessions established with the Control Board, the organization was now able to concentrate on the eighteen-month drive to the founding convention on May 28, 1996. In those eighteen months, the leaders conducted over fifteen hundred individual meetings, two hundred and fifty house meetings, and numerous research actions to figure out how to turn the "problems" we were hearing about into concrete "issues" that the organization could take action on.

This long but necessary and revelatory process allowed the organization to develop an initial action-ready agenda and a core of primary leaders. Throughout the process—even though some early leaders became impatient to "get going"—new people coming together from all parts of the city and the research actions they were doing together actually provided the glue and the confidence needed to found a powerful organization.

During this long process, not only the Control Board but also Mayor Barry, some city council members, and a number of business leaders worked to throw sand into WIN's progress. For example, the year before the founding, WIN held a 900-member meeting to hear from one another regarding the issues that were emerging from our house meetings campaign. Mayor Barry was invited to the meeting and arrived fifteen minutes late so he could disrupt the meeting by walking down the aisle shaking everybody's hand. When he got to the front of the room where the leaders and I were gathered, he walked up to Rev. Daniels and, pointing to me, said loudly, "Who is this honky running the show?" Rev. Daniels replied matter-of-factly, "He works for us. Please take your seat Mr. Mayor." This is how it went with Mayor Barry, because the ties that bound the leaders and me through two years of consistent relationship building were too strong for even the popular and clever mayor to break.

Jonetta Rose Barras, a very astute and savvy reporter at the time, recently told me that WIN not only survived but thrived because "WIN was not captured by the traditional old timers. WIN was large, racially and economically diverse, and those three young African American pastors would not be intimidated by the powers that be."

She went on to say, "Most politicians did not know what to do with WIN. Actually, most of them did not think that WIN would last and responded in a patronizing way when they talked about WIN."

After over three years of slow, respectful work over twenty-one-hundred leaders from fifty congregations, from every ward in the city, formally had their founding assembly and unveiled an initial issues agenda. As I sat watching the meeting unfold, I felt deep admiration for what the leaders had accomplished. Even Mayor Barry, who had tried to dereail WIN, publicly stated at the meeting that he had never seen such a disciplined large crowd come together from every ward in the city. Watching the leaders operate at such a high level of politics, I could feel tears of joy filling my eyes.

I knew that many difficult and trying times lie ahead for WIN, but for one moment it felt like another night very close to the world as it should be.

FIVE

A DIVIDE
ON THE COMMONS

The phone rang early one morning in 2004, startling me into semi-consciousness. As I fumbled to pick up the phone, I could hear Cheri Andes' voice asking me excitedly if I had seen the *Boston Globe*'s front-page story.

When I finally gathered myself, I asked her why she sounded so frantic. She told me to get my computer and read the article on the demonstration that took place on the Boston Commons the day before. She added, "I think we are dead! The issue of equal marriage will tear us apart."

Cheri was the very talented lead organizer of the Greater Boston Interfaith Organization (GBIO), and I was the Industrial Areas Foundation (IAF) national supervisor working with her and the organization. The State Supreme Court had issued a ruling requiring the Massachusetts State Legislature to change the wording of the law on marriage to recognize same-sex marriages. Demonstrators on both sides of the issue were separated by a rope line, surrounded by police, and yelling at each other. Rev. Jennifer Mills Knutson, the Associate Pastor of Old South Church and GBIO's co-chair, was quoted in the *Boston Globe* article as saying that the issue of equal marriage was a civil rights issue. Rev. Hurman Hamilton, the African American pastor of Roxbury Presbyterian Church, the other co-chair of GBIO, was quoted as saying that passing a law legalizing same-sex marriage was wrong. (Fortunately for the organization, the reporter did not mention the fact that Revs. Knutson and Hamilton were the co-chairs of GBIO.)

At the time when the issue of equal marriage burst on the scene, GBIO was in a very fragile state of existence. The two excellent founding co-lead organizers,

Jim Drake and Lew Finfer, were gone. Cheri Andes
had recently become the lead organizer and was just
beginning to establish herself in that position. Additionally, many of the Roman Catholic parishes that
comprised a majority of the founding congregations
were being forced to either close or merge with other parishes. Additionally, the all-powerful mayor of
Boston, Thomas Menino, hated GBIO. (When I was
first introduced to him, he called GBIO The Greater
Boston Idiots Organization). Finally, as hard as Jim,
Lew, and the leaders had worked to diversify the
organization, GBIO had remained predominately
white.

In 2003, I had worked as the interim lead organizer—traveling from my home in Maryland to
live in Boston every other week. I understood my
role as re-building the organization, developing the
new lead organizer, and diversifying the base of the
organization.

During that year, through the very fine work of
GBIO's associate organizer, Ari Lipman, we slowly
began to bring in a number of Haitian congrega-

tions. I concentrated on recruiting African American congregations in addition to conducting numerous training sessions and discussions with the primary leaders of GBIO.

As this work progressed, we slowly began to change the issues agenda, the base of the organization, and the mix of people in leadership positions. By 2004, a clear pathway for success was becoming evident. Then the issue of equal marriage exploded, threatening to split the organization in two.

Many of the white leaders were adamantly in support of equal marriage, while virtually all of the Haitian and African American leaders were adamantly opposed to it. I shared Cheri's fears about GBIO's future. It was definitely unclear whether these newly formed and still fragile relationships within GBIO would withstand the strong feelings that people on both sides of the issues expressed.

Soon after the front-page article appeared in *The Globe*, some powerful African American clergy, led by Bishop Gilbert Thompson, the pastor of a mega-church not connected with GBIO, called for a rally to oppose equal marriage. Over 2000 Black clergy and lay people attended the rally. Bishop Thompson was the main speaker. His talk included some very ugly and inflammatory comments. Rev. Hamilton also spoke at the rally. His comments centered around his opposition of equal marriage from his theological point of view. The reporter from the *Boston Globe* who attended the rally quoted only Bishop Thompson's incendiary comments. The reporting of the bishop's comments brought the emotions from the pro-equal-marriage proponents to a fever pitch. It certainly did not help

The issues seemed to futher expose an already deep historical divide between the African American and white communities.

that the issues seemed to further expose an already deep historical divide between the African American and other religious communities.

The day the article appeared, Rev. Hamilton realized that the emotions he had helped light threatened the very existence of GBIO. That morning, he called his co-chair Rev. Knutsen, who he knew was pro-equal marriage, to come and talk. Rev. Knutsen agreed that they needed to meet to discuss what was needed to do to ensure GBIO's survival.

When Rev. Hamilton called Cheri Andes to inform her about his initiating a meeting with Rev. Knutsen, Cheri tried to talk him out of meeting her alone. She knew where both stood on the issues. She also knew that Rev. Hamilton's relationship with Rev. Knutsen was new and she feared that if their meeting went poorly GBIO's future would be in serious jeopardy. Cheri called me to see if I would intervene with Rev. Hamilton to dissuade him from meeting with Rev. Knutsen alone. I fully understood Cheri's concerns and why she called me.

Rev. Hamilton and I had begun to develop a very close and trusting relationship. Although he was one of very few African American pastors present at the founding of GBIO, by the time I arrived on the scene his activity in the organization had waned. As the pastor of a small, struggling, African American Presbyterian Church in the Roxbury section of Boston, he had decided to dedicate all of his energy into the building of the congregation.

When I did my first individual meeting with Rev. Hamilton, I felt an immediate connection with him. He may have had only 40 to 50 members at that time, but there was something very special about him. Beyond his keen intellect, he radiated a positive spirit. Usually, I try to keep an initial face-to-face individual meeting with a new potential leader to around 45 minutes. After what seemed like 30 minutes to me, I realized that I had been in his office for an hour and a half. From then on, Rev. Hamilton and I met with each other frequently. Eventually, he became the President of GBIO, after Rev. Knutsen left Boston to pastor another church.

Rev. Hamilton's political savvy grew exponentially. Eventually, he became a major figure in Boston and Massachusetts politics as GBIO's president—never forgetting to bring other leaders along with him, both figuratively and literally. His leadership played a major role in the organization's rise in political recognition, esteem, and success. Even though he now pastors a large non-denominational congregation in California, the memory of his leadership and his imprint on GBIO remain vivid to this day.

When Cheri called me to intervene with Rev. Hamilton, I told her that while I completely understood her concerns, I thought that we should trust his instincts; besides, he had already set up the meeting with Rev. Knutsen.

The two ministers knew that they stood on opposite sides of the issue of equal marriage, but they were absolutely together on the importance of the survival of GBIO—especially as it was just becoming appropriately broad-based and diverse.

One of the foundational universal principles that Saul Alinsky and Ed Chambers and Dick Harmon and others taught all of us IAF organizers was the primary importance of the face-to-face individual meeting. They called it the most radical tool in the organizer's arsenal.

The individual meeting is a 30-45-minute, face-to-face encounter. Its purpose is for both participants to explore each other's story, to see if there might be a mutual self-interest on which they could consider acting together. It is not an "interview," and it is not an attempt to pry into someone's private life; it is a discussion meant to determine if there is a basis of trust to engage in public action together. After 45 years of engaging literally thousands of people in this way, I can attest to the power and the radical nature that are inherent in the individual one-to-one relational meeting.

The individual meeting is meant to determine is there is a basis of trust to engage in public action together.

Rev. Hamilton and Rev. Knutsen had been with GBIO long enough to have discovered and explored the power of quality individual meetings. Their agreement to meet face-to-face at that crucial moment was spot on. If they had not previously met in this manner to establish a relationship of respect and trust, their meeting at such a charged time would have been either a waste of time or an unmitigated disaster. Instead, each minister engaged the other without trying to convince the other that his or her position was the right one. They started from the basis of respect for each other and in the common belief that, in the long run, the Boston metropolitan area badly needed a broadly based, diverse, non-partisan organization such as GBIO.

Their meeting concluded with a decision: They would convene a small group of leaders who were on opposite sides of the equal marriage issue to explore—without organizing staff present, by the way—ways to move through the existential crisis facing GBIO. They invited Rabbi Jonah Pesner, Rev. Wesley Roberts, Rev. David Carl Olsen, and Rev.

Ray Hammond to join them to discuss how GBIO should move forward.

When Rev. Hamilton told Cheri Andes about their decision, she once again became very anxious, which was understandable given the gravity of the split. Rabbi Jonah Pesner, who was the associate rabbi at Temple Israel, a member congregation of GBIO and a very large and prominent synagogue in the Boston region, had just begun to become involved in GBIO through the urging of Fran Godine, a wonderful lay leader at Temple Israel.

While the senior rabbi at Temple Israel, Ron Freidman, was a strong supporter of GBIO, he had numerous responsibilities that kept him from becoming a senior leader in GBIO. At Ms. Godine's and Rabbi Freidman's urging, Rabbi Pesner had begun to become more involved in the organization.

Rabbi Pesner, who is now the executive director of the Religious Action Center of the Union of Reformed Judaism, was a young, smart, engaging, charismatic leader. He exuded energy and enthusiasm. Along with GBIO organizers, he and other

Jewish leaders had assisted in recruiting additional synagogues into the organization. Today, there are 14 dues-paying synagogues that belong to GBIO.

Temple Israel was and is an open, affirming synagogue that has a number of gay couples as part of their membership. The temple's rabbis and membership were publicly supportive of the Equal Marriage Movement. Rev. Ray Hammond was and still is the pastor of Bethel A.M.E. Church in Boston. I have always thought of Rev. Hammond as a true renaissance man because his interests are so varied and fascinating. He was born and raised in Philadelphia, entered Harvard at the age of 16, and at age 24 graduated Harvard Medical School. After practicing medicine for many years, he responded to God's call to become a full-time minister.

Every organizer that had ever worked for GBIO had tried to recruit Rev. Hammond. The reasons for this were obvious. He is not only a fine pastor, but from the very beginning of his ministry he has been deeply engaged in the community. He was one of the co-founders of the 10 Point Coalition—an organization that was widely recognized as turning around a terrible spike of homicides in the African American community. There was no local or state politician, including Mayor Menino, who did not hold Rev. Hammond in the highest regard.

It was never the case that Rev. Hammond did not respect GBIO's work; he was so busy with many other organizations, such as the 10 Point Coalition and other endeavors in the Black community, that he did not understand why his general support on various GBIO issues, such as affordable housing, was not sufficient. Cheri and I, along with many leaders in GBIO, knew that Bethel Church's joining would bring instant credibility to GBIO's re-organizing efforts. After meeting with Rev. Hammond numerous times and with the help of Rev. Hamilton, GBIO brought Bethel A.M.E. into the organization as a dues-paying member just before the Marriage Equality issue exploded.

Five of the six ministers invited met and decided to make two recommendations: First, to call for an expanded GBIO leaders meeting; and second, to recommend to the leaders that GBIO agree to take no public stand on the issue of equal marriage. They also agreed to ask each leader to make clear when and if asked to speak publicly on the issue that they would be clear that they were speaking as an individual—not as a GBIO leader. (Eventually, Bishop Thompson, who had only recently joined GBIO, left the organization based on this decision.)

In between the small group meeting and the proposed leader's meeting, Rabbi Pesner called Rev. Hamilton with an invitation. He asked if the minister and Rev. Hammond would be willing to come to dinner hosted by two gay couples from Temple Israel at one of the couple's homes. Rabbi Pesner said that if the two ministers agreed, he and Rabbi Freidman would join everyone for dinner.

Rabbi Pesner explained that these two couples had been very impressed with both Rev. Hamilton and Rev. Hammond at GBIO meetings but now wanted Rabbi Freidman to pull Temple Israel out of GBIO due to the pastors' opposition to equal marriage. The two rabbis had come up with the idea for this dinner and convinced the two couples that this invitation was the right course of action to pursue.

Rev. Hamilton immediately agreed and said that he would contact Rev. Hammond, who did not hesitate in accepting the invitation. Cheri Andes was convinced that this was a terrible idea. She knew correctly that neither man would ever change his mind on this volatile issue. She also had never met the gay couples who were hosting the dinner. This, plus her knowledge of Rabbi Pesner's passionate belief in equal marriage rights, increased her concerns.

In talking to Rev. Hammond recently about the dinner, he said that he completely understood Cheri's trepidations. First, he was a new member of GBIO, and Cheri had not gotten to know him very well. Second, neither Cheri nor he nor Rev. Hamilton knew who these two couples were. Rev. Hammond told me that he had a sense that if everyone did not come to the dinner with an open heart and open mind, the entire endeavor would be a disaster.

The dinner lasted about two hours. According to the participants there was very little conversation about the issue of equal marriage. As Rev. Hammond and Rabbi Pesner recounted the story to me, everyone spent their time together sharing stories about significant events that had shaped their lives.

The dinner had a profound impact on Rev. Hamilton's life.

Rev. Hamilton said that the evening had a profound impact on his life. He left the dinner believing that a concrete wall had been replaced by a spirit of understanding and mutual respect. Rev. Hammond told me, "The wall turned into an open doorway."

I was greatly moved, as was Cheri Andes, by what these leaders had risked and learned about themselves and the others at the dinner. As Cheri told me later, "The leaders saved the organization."

The belief in building relationships of trust across various boundaries of differences had been completely affirmed. I was grateful to the IAF relational culture that I had learned from my first men-tors at the IAF. This learning had been constantly reinforced over and again at national and local training sessions, and that ultimately gave me the courage to believe that it might work even in this explosive situation.

A couple of weeks later when the extended leaders meeting took place, although there was some palpable tension in the room, I was confident that Rev. Hamilton, Rev. Hammond, Rev. Knutsen, Rev. Olsen, and Rabbi Pesner would carry the day.

Even though Cheri had briefed other leaders prior to the meeting, there was still some uncertainty as to how the proposal would be received. Knutsen and Hamilton laid out the idea that GBIO would formally take no position on the issue of marriage equality. This was met with complete silence. It was difficult to discern what the silence meant. However, after Rev. Hamilton told the story about the dinner he and a few of the leaders had attended at the gay couple's home and how the event had a profound effect on all in attendance, almost everyone began to talk. The more people spoke, the more it became evident that good will was developing in the room.

Eventually, a vote was taken and passed unanimously to accept the recommendations that had been put forward by the clergy leaders. The organization survived and thrived because of that decision to avoid an issue that was internally divisive. (After this meeting, Revs. Hamilton and Hammond decided on their own to never again speak publicly on this issue—not even as individuals.)

A couple of months later, 450 members of GBIO met at Salem Seventh Day Adventist Church. Salem is a large Haitian church in the Mattapan neighborhood of Boston and had originally been a synagogue. In fact, there was still a large Star of David at the top of the front door entrance.

At this action, GBIO had the State's Attorney

General present to publicly pledge to uphold a civil rights agenda developed by GBIO leaders and Certified Nursing Home Assistants (CNA) workers from the Haitian churches.

In doing hundreds of individual meetings and house meetings in synagogues and Haitian churches, leaders and organizers had heard myriad stories and complaints. From the Jewish community, there was a good deal of frustration and anger about the poor care their parents and relatives were receiving at various nursing homes. From the Haitian community, there was a good deal of frustration among Haitian CNA workers who were being mistreated by owners of nursing homes. (We had learned that many nursing homes assigned 20 or more beds to each CNA to clean each day in violation of Massachusetts State regulations. We also learned that at break times, and in violation of their civil rights, CNA workers were forbidden to speak Creole, their native tongue.)

Given this situation, GBIO initiated a series of house meetings involving Jewish and Haitian leaders who belonged to GBIO. At these meetings, leaders from both communities exchanged stories and frustrations. Together, they concluded that the root of the problem stemmed from the bad behavior of nursing-home owners. Relationship building led the two communities to develop a workers' civil rights agenda to present to the Massachusetts State Attorney General.

At one point, one of the major nursing-home owners—who belonged to Temple Israel—went to Rabbi Freidman to ask him to intervene with GBIO on his behalf. After all, he was a member of the Temple in good standing and a generous contributor. When he brought his request to Rabbi Freidman, the rabbi told him that he would do no such thing. He reminded the nursing-home owner the meaning of Jewish ethics and values. Rabbi Freidman asked the owner to live out his faith. Once again, Rabbi Freidman showed how a principled and upright leader should act.

On the wonderful night of that action at Salem Seventh Day Adventist Church, the State's Attorney agreed to act on the agreement that was brought to him by GBIO.

Three months before this action, GBIO would not have been able to hold such an action at Salem because Temple Israel and the Haitian church factions were still deeply divided on the equal marriage issue. However, newborn trust and respect had evolved, and the two communities and the entire organization were able to move forward to correct a serious injustice.

The power and symbolism of this meeting taking place at a Haitian church that was originally a synagogue; where a local union had been founded in its basement; where the grandfather of Ari Lipman, the Jewish GBIO associate organizer who had brought Salem into GBIO, were recognized by all the leaders who had taken the organization through the storm that had almost destroyed its very existence.

Newborn trust and respect had evolved.

Today, among many other victories, GBIO has successfully pushed the Commonwealth of Massachusetts to pass legislation for universal health care; criminal justice reform; and the establishment of a $70 million public STEM school in Roxbury, among other victories.

SIX

LEAVING THE PARTY TOO SOON

I have had two reactions to my encounters with machine mayors while organizing in Chicago and Milwaukee under the reigns of Mayor Richard J. Daley (the first Mayor Daley) and Mayor Henry Maier, respectively. One reaction was one of complete disgust. Both mayors fostered corruption and distributed favors for those who supported them. The second reaction has been a sustained curiosity as to what machine politics could achieve if it stood for the whole instead of the few. Late in my career I got a chance to find out, albeit in another country.

That is why when my good friend and colleague Jonathan Lange called me in the Fall of 2010 with a proposition, I was intrigued, but also dismissive at first.

Jonathan is as creative an organizer as there is.

While he was working for the BUILD organization, he developed and organized the passage of the first Living Wage Ordinance in the country in 1994. Soon after this success in Baltimore, the IAF organization in New York City followed suit and pushed the New York City Council to pass the second Living Wage law. Since then, over 100 jurisdictions in the United States have passed similar legislation.

During this time, Jonathan was also working with the IAF partner organization in London called Citizens UK, which had been founded by Neil Jamieson after he had spent time in Chicago with Ed Chambers and in New York City with Mike Gecan, both with the national Industrial Areas Foundation (IAF)

Jonathan had spent two-three weeks three or four times a year working with Mr. Jamieson and his staff for over ten years. On his return from his trip to the UK in October 2010, Jonathan called me, starting his conversation with, "Arnie, don't dismiss this idea out of hand." (Not a great opening when you are trying to recruit someone, but it worked this time.)

He told me that the newly elected leader of the Labour Party was Ed Miliband, and Miliband had just made Maurice Glasman, a university professor and a Citizens UK leader, a Lord. Jonathan knew Maurice well, because he had been a leader in Citizens UK's efforts to establish a living wage law in London.

I had met Maurice Glasman only once when I and about 20 Metro IAF leaders traveled to London to celebrate Citizen UK's 10th anniversary. We had met for about an hour for an interview he did of me for a book that he was writing. I remembered Maurice because he was insightful, funny, and warm hearted. On Jonathan's trip to London in the fall of 2010, Maurice told Jonathan that, in his view, Ed Miliband was young and inexperienced. What Ed needed, Maurice believed, was a mentor. Maurice asked Jonathan to have me taking up this role.

I told Jonathan that, while he had many terrific ideas, this one was just plain crazy!

First, I knew nothing about British politics or the Labour Party. Second, given that Ed Miliband knew nothing about me or this idea, **I knew nothing about British politics or the Labour Party.** Maurice's suggestion seemed ridiculous. Third, I reminded Jonathan that my elderly mother was living with my wife and me and was under our care because she had broken her hip and was unable to care for herself.

Soon after I spoke with Jonathan, however, Maurice called me from London. He put a hard sell on me and admitted that Ed Miliband knew nothing about this idea. "Maurice," I said, "How can I mentor someone whom I have never met and who has no idea of what you are scheming?"

Maurice was undeterred. The fact that Miliband did not know of my existence did not seem to matter to Maurice at all. In fact, except for the one time I met with Maurice years earlier, he and I did not know each other either. When I reminded Maurice of these facts, he simply replied that his intuition about me and my reputation was all he needed to know. "Ed Miliband needs a mentor, and you are the exact right person to do this."

After turning down Maurice's offer two more times, he proposed that I come to London for ten days to meet with some Labour MPs and Ed Miliband so that I could offer him my best advice on how to move forward as the new leader of the Labour Party. Talk about baiting a fish and reeling it in. How could I resist such an interesting "one-time-only" experience?

In December 2010, I arrived in London for what became a fascinating ten days of meetings with MPs, journalists, Labour Party staff, interesting political thinkers...and Ed Miliband. My first meeting with Ed's brother, David, was very delicate. David Miliband had been the presumptive candidate to lead the Labour Party after Gordon Brown stepped down from being the leader of the party. David had held many senior positions in the government when Labour led the country, and the last position he held was that of Foreign Secretary (akin to our Secretary of State).

At the last minute, Ed Miliband had decided to run against his own brother for leader of the Labour Party. Ed, to many people's surprise, beat his brother in a close race with the strong support of the trade unions. Today, David lives in the US and is the president of the International Rescue Committee. I met with David twice over the course of ten days. He was very cordial towards me, but the anger he felt towards his brother was palpable.

Since Maurice set up meetings with very interesting people, the ten days seemed to fly by. My last scheduled meeting—and my first with the new head of the Labour Party—was with Ed Miliband himself. Maurice had kept Ed abreast of all the people with whom I had been meeting, but he also kept me from the new Labour leader until I had met with everyone else, including Ed's disgruntled brother.

So by the time I met with Ed Miliband, I had spent a good deal of time reflecting with Maurice on what I was learning from the many people I had met. I found myself becoming more intrigued with the idea of exploring a working relationship with Ed and the Labour Party. That relationship was so close during those years that I will refer to Miliband by his first name throughout this chapter.

The proposal I developed was to ask Ed Miliband to invite me to return to the UK in the summer for six weeks of travel in order to personally meet with Labour and civic leaders throughout the country, at the end of which time I would write a report to him on my reflections and suggestions.

When I entered Ed's conference room to meet with him for the first time, the view from where I was asked to sit was of Big Ben. I could not fathom that I was there to meet with the man who in five years could well be the Prime Minister of the UK.

Ed was friendly, relaxed, and very easy to talk to. He asked me for my reflections on my meetings so far. I told him that obviously ten days of meetings, all taking place in London with mostly Members of Parliament, had left me far from being an expert in much of anything. But I told him I had developed one thought. The Labour Party, I had concluded, did things backwards. It made its decisions from the top to bottom instead of from the bottom to the top as we do in the IAF. It appeared to me that the membership had very little input into the major decisions the Party made.

Ed Miliband wanted to make the Living Wage idea part of Labour's manifesto.

Ed listened attentively, and then surprised me by agreeing with me without reservation. Being curious and supportive of the Living Wage idea, he asked me how I had come up with the idea. He said he wanted to make it part of Labour's manifesto and wanted the name of the professor or think tank that had developed the idea.

I proceeded to tell Ed the story of Jonathan Lange's meetings with hundreds of low-wage workers in Baltimore so that he could learn what life was like for them. I said it was through hundreds of individual and small group meetings that Jonathan and the low-wage workers had developed the "Living Wage" campaign together. Ed seemed taken by the idea that Jonathan and low-wage workers had developed this plan and not some expert or group of experts.

After further discussion with Ed, I proposed spending six weeks meeting with Labour and civic leaders throughout the UK. I said that I would like to do this without media and without either his or other Labour leaders joining me. Ed liked the idea, and he called his staff to meet me and tell them of our agreement. Although they were not pleased that there would be no press coverage, my return was set up for six weeks beginning in June 2011.

I was not sure what the six weeks would produce, if anything, but I was excited to return five months later. Meanwhile, I returned home to the U.S. and my wife, Lucile, and I worked out a plan with my mom while I would be gone.

On my return to London, my first task was to gain the trust of the party staff; particularly some of the regional party directors who resided and ran Labour's field operations throughout the country. Thus my first two weeks were spent meeting with regional directors and their staff. The directors were understandably mistrustful of me. First, they were constantly subjected to multiple "experts" foisted upon them by their leaders in London. This meant that their work was constantly being interrupted to accommodate "visitors," which is how they initially viewed me. Second, they often had to host Labour Shadow Cabinet leaders who wanted to give a speech in their "patch." Arranging these events often took 3-5 days of preparation time for the regional staff. Third, what did an American know about British politics that could be useful to them?

These were all legitimate concerns, so instead of dispensing advice upon my arrival in the various regions, I asked the directors if I could go with their organizers and their team of leaders as they went door-to-door to campaign for local council elections.

This request intrigued many of the regional directors, organizers, and local leaders, partly because it was so different from the usual requests from visitors from "London."

In my time with the IAF, I have knocked on thousands of doors during our non-partisan Get Out The Vote (GOTV) drives. The difference in the UK was that this time I was knocking on doors for an actual partisan political party. It was a different experience for me.

At first, I simply observed how the party members and organizers spoke to people at the door. After a bit, I asked the organizers if I could initiate some conversations with people. Everyone agreed to my request, as there is a certain camaraderie that develops on a team of door knockers as they move from street to street. Whether you are in the USA or the UK, door knocking is door knocking. You do not have a long time to spend at

Whether you are in the USA or the UK, door knocking is door knocking.

each house or apartment. You are working to identify people as "strong" or "mild" supporters, "undecideds," or "forget about them."

Labour door knockers spent between 30-60 seconds at a person's door. This allowed very little time for any type of conversation. When I knocked, I tried to engage people for several minutes in a way that enabled me to connect with them in a real way. At one point, after gaining some trust with some of my fellow door-knockers, I asked our team to walk up one side of the street and down the other side of the street and just observe what they saw. I think they agreed to do so just to humor me.

When we finished, I gathered them for a conversation about what they had seen. Some saw nothing but houses, but others observed bicycles in some yards, flower gardens, and organizational stickers on some doors. I suggested that starting with what they observed was a good way to initiate a discussion at the doors.

As the door knockers began to follow this simple suggestion, most were pleasantly surprised that about one in every five people they encountered opened up to them briefly about their interests. This meant that the canvassers not only learned what issues were on people's minds but were also able to recruit some people to pass out literature to friends, to work a phone bank for the Labour Party, and in some cases even to even "door knock" their own street and neighborhood. (Of course, having people canvass their own streets and neighborhoods is much more effective than "outsiders" doing it.)

In addition to participating in door knocking, I met individually and in small groups throughout the country with local Labour leaders, council members, and organizers, as well as other civic leaders. By the end of my six-week trip, I had met with 1,011 people—either individually or in small groups of 8 to15 people.

I kept a careful record of what I was learning throughout my trip. My report highlighted a few things:

1) Organizers were organizers in name only. The majority of their time was spent in internal meetings, resolving internal disputes, and door knocking for election support. Given that in a five-year cycle there are as many four elections (local, county, national), the "organizers" have little time for actual organizing.

2) The organizers had very little time or incentive to meet with civic and business leaders not already committed to the Labour Party. Additionally, many organizers in one area were moved for two-to-three months to work on local elections throughout the country. As a result, many of them did not have any analysis of the power patterns on the ground in the areas they were temporarily assigned to. One of the results of all this was a high turnover of organizers, who were viewed as low people on the totem pole by the Labour Party.

3) The level of disconnect between London and the field staff was filled by large doses of resentment.

4) Finally, there was a complete absence of any vision animating the work in the field beyond that of defeating the Tory Party in the next election.

I concluded my report by stating that the over-whelming victory of the Tory Prime Minister David Cameron in 2010 and the residue of negative feelings from the battle between Ed Miliband and his brother had resulted in a fatigued Labour Party, especially in the regions outside London.

When I met with Ed to discuss my report, he expressed his appreciation for the breadth and depth of my travels, work and observations. My recommendations to him centered on training organizers to actually be organizers. To do this, Labour would need to conduct numerous training sessions for the staff in the field aimed at redefining the role and work of the organizers in the Party.

Ed was interested in my recommendations and asked me about my availability to spend time in the country to conduct training sessions with the staff in the field and to implement some of my ideas. We concluded our meeting with me agreeing to spend three weeks every quarter for the years 2011 and 2012. In addition to training sessions, I agreed to meet with MPs, Ed's staff, and some of his "Shadow Cabinet" members to introduce them to some of my ideas and to what I was learning from meeting with so many people throughout England, Scotland, and Wales.

To have any chance of success, I needed to gain the support of the newly elected General Secretary, Iain McNicol, who was the director of the entire Labour Party staff. Iain had defeated Ed Miliband's choice for this position. This illustrated some of Ed's deep problems within the party, and given this situation, I was wondering if Iain would support me. But it turned out that Iain, who now sits in the House of Lords, is a wonderful person and was fully on board with my assignment. He never wavered in support of me and what I was attempting to accomplish.

Additionally, I was very fortunate that the two main Labour Party staff people for training, Tom Geldard and Jenny Bettenridge, were open to, supportive of, and very competent in executing the plan. We formed a good team.

Beginning in 2012, Ed suggested that Tom, Jenny, and I expand our training to work with Labour's proposed MP candidates who would be running in the 2015 general election. We were glad to do so. By then, I was all in. I loved the challenge of figuring out how to modify my IAF organizing workshops to develop new training sessions that incorporated United Kingdom realities. In 2012, I stepped down from being a co-director of the IAF so that there would not be a conflict with the IAF's 501(c) (3) non-partisan tax status.

I loved the challenge of figuring out how to develop new workshops that incorporated UK realities.

Although physically tired at times, I felt renewed. I was grateful to have a brand-new opportunity to use my past experiences on behalf of an entirely new cause. I think that my longtime IAF colleagues, Jonathan Lange and Mike Gecan, intuited this when they encouraged me to take this opportunity and run with it.

Throughout 2012, Tom, Jenny, and I travelled extensively conducting training sessions. By doing this and continuing my travels throughout the UK to meet with Labour leaders and staff, as well as outside civic leaders, I continued to hone my ideas on what it would take to begin to turn around the Labour Party's fortunes.

As I did this, I was asked to make numerous presentations to local party members, Members of Parliament, and to lecture at Oxford and other universities. This work forced me to become more precise in my thinking about how to present IAF's organizing principles in a totally different context. I discovered that most of the universals translated easily to other contexts.

Throughout this time, I was very fortunate to have some wonderful people like Marc Stears, Ed's speech writer; Tom Baldwin, Ed's political staffer; Jon Cruddas and Tessa Jowell, two very different but wonderful MPs; and brilliant Labour thinkers like Jonathan Rutherford and Scott Langdon to feed me personally and intellectually. And, of course, Maurice

Glasman, who became my dearest friend, thought reflector, and schemer in the UK. Maurice and his wonderful wife, Catherine, and their four terrific children, became my family away from home.

Most importantly, Ed Miliband and I would meet every time I came to London. Sometimes, I travelled with him by train to wherever he was going; and sometimes we met in his London office. However, the most productive meetings we had were those that took place in his home, as there were no distractions or interruptions there.

As 2013 approached, Ed told me that it was time to put my training into action. The place to do that was in the approaching 2013 elections.

I knew that he was right, and so I began to reflect on where to try out my ideas. The 2013 local elections did not include the entire United Kingdom, but they did include Lancashire County, which has the second largest unitary County Council in England.

This was fortunate for me, because the regional director for Labour was Anna Hutchinson. Anna is a very bright and warm-hearted person who had amassed a hard-working, talented staff that were not intimidated by new ideas. I thought highly of them and appreciated their ideas and the time they had taken with me to teach me about the areas they worked in.

Lancashire County in the election of 2009 had gone Tory in a big way. From formerly controlling the County Council, Labour had been trounced in the election of 2009. Of the 86 County Council seats, Labour had won only 17. Because of this, Anna and her organizers were open to new ideas to see if this new political reality could be turned around. The idea of winning 43 seats to regain the majority seemed unlikely, but Anna hoped that Labour could at least cut into the Tory's majority by a decent number.

Anna asked Noel Hutchison, her husband, who was an organizer on her staff, to lead the campaign. I liked Noel a great deal because he is smart, hard-working, funny, and willing to swing for the fences. When I had asked Anna if I could work with her team, she said it would be fine with her, but only if her team agreed to do so. After meeting with the staff, there was agreement to proceed.

As the 2013 election approached, I increased my time in the UK, spending every other month there. I told Ed that I would focus my time on the Lancashire election and the training of the Labour MP candidates running for the 2015 general election.

I asked Ed to allow members of the local Lancashire Party to establish their own manifesto.

Given Anna's agreement for me to work on the Lancashire election, I had only one request of Ed. I asked him to allow the members of the local Lancashire Party to establish their own manifesto (issue agenda).

Generally, the national leadership of the party to my way of thinking had too much influence in deciding a local party's manifesto. If some of my ideas were to be allowed to be tried out, Ed had to agree to local control of their own campaign. With his agreement to my request, I began to work with Noel and his staff on the campaign.

There were a few ideas I took from my past IAF experiences that I believed we had to do:

1) There had to be broad ownership by everyone working on the campaign about the development of the manifesto.

2) There had to be hundreds of individual meetings with Party members and non-Party members to learn the most important issues that we should campaign on.

3) We needed to include conversations with non-Party members so we could increase low propensity voters to vote.

4) We had to gain a buy-in from the local Labour leader, Jenny Mein, and her supporters to this approach.

5) We needed to be flexible.

Approximately seven months before election day, Noel gathered eleven Party leaders at my request so I could conduct a training session on our suggested approach and on how to conduct individual relationship meetings.

At the end of the session, I asked each Party leader to commit to conducting ten individual meetings over the next eight weeks with community leaders they knew; with the goal of each person bringing at least five people to the next meeting.

Two weeks before the date of the meeting, Noel reported that he expected at least 65 people to be in attendance. Noel, a few leaders, and I planned out the second meeting's agenda, which was to take place at a local Hindu Temple. When I arrived at the Temple, the room was abuzz. By the time we started the meeting, there were 109 people in attendance. Noel, particularly, was pleased because his role had not involved delivering the turn-out. His staff and the leaders had produced, and he could praise them for their good work.

After some initial talks emphasizing that the local manifesto would be decided by them, we broke up the participants into groups of ten. We encouraged people to sit with people from different areas of Lancashire County. Noel and I led two of the ten groups. The others were led by leaders.

At the tables, each participant was asked to introduce himself or herself, state where they lived in the county, and to name their top five concerns. A thirty-minute discussion ensued after which everyone wrote down five issues they wanted to become the core of the manifesto. At the end of this process, we took a 15-minute break so that the top issues could be tabulated. The buzz in the room during the break was music to my ears. After the five top issues were announced, we asked each person in the room to bring one other person to the next meeting for a ratification vote. After this proposal was voted upon unanimously, the meeting was adjourned. The room did not empty for a long time as people lingered to talk and hang out, which is always a good sign in organizing.

Ed Miliband sent a key ally of his, Jon Trickett, an MP from another constituency, to attend the meeting. Trickett approached me to say how enthusiastic he felt about the meeting. Although I did not know he would be there, I was very pleased that he would take back a good report to Ed.

As the date for the second meeting began to approach, Noel and I became very concerned about the forecast for snow in Lancashire County. Noel had secured a large room that was attached to the Preston Football Stadium to accommodate our expected attendance of 200 people. We both knew our effort was hopeful but fragile. We were concerned that if the weather forced us to cancel the meeting, we would lose the excitement that had been generated at the first meeting. We grappled with whether to postpone the meeting and set a new date, but as the forecast was uncertain we decided to go forward as planned.

We both knew our effort was hopeful but fragile.

On the day of the second meeting, snow was falling at a heavy clip as my train from London rolled into Preston. When I arrived at the meeting place, Noel was nervous. He had received numerous cancellation calls. I felt my heart sinking into my stomach. But by 7:00 pm, we had about 90 people in attendance. Given the snowstorm, this was an excellent turnout, but not what we believed we needed. Regardless, we went forward. After some discussion, the proposed manifesto was passed with a near unanimous vote. At the end of the meeting, everyone determined that we needed at least 200 people at a *third* meeting to kick-off the campaign to elect a Labour Council. We would invite Ed Miliband as the head of the Party to speak. People left the meeting hopeful but unsure about our chances for success.

I knew if this effort was a failure, my time in the UK would be over. The train ride back to my apartment in London the next morning seemed to take forever. I felt as uneasy and uncertain as I had ever felt about my work in the UK, unsure of what would transpire next. Would Ed come to Preston for the meeting? Would 200 people show up? If 200 people did not show and Ed and his staff came, I believed that my time in the UK would end.

When I returned to the UK a week before the third meeting as scheduled, I was met by a phone call from Noel. He told me that turnout was not looking good. He said he had only thirty people committed to attend the meeting. We were obviously in trouble. It seemed clear that we had lost the excitement people had expressed at our first meeting. We had no choice but to double down in our effort to turn out a good crowd. The only recourse we had was to meet with the eleven original leaders—which we did—and tell them that our effort would either sink or swim based on the success of the third meeting. We needed them to triple their efforts.

Three days before the meeting, Noel called to tell me that a miracle was taking place. We were oversubscribed! Within four days, the leaders had called in with over 300 commitments. Eleven leaders and Noel had taken us from 30 to over 300 people. I was elated; but still Noel was nervous. He said the fire code prevented that many people in the meeting room and we would need to tell some people not to come. I told him that in my entire career I had never uninvited anyone to attend a meeting. Never!

Noel was understandably concerned that with Ed there, if the Fire Department forced people to leave, there would be chaos; nevertheless, we chose potential chaos over telling people not to come.

On the day of the meeting, I travelled by train with Ed and his staff from Carlyle to Preston. Ed had given a talk in Carlyle that was well received, and he seemed excited as the train approached Preston. When we arrived at the Preston meeting hall, about an hour before the meeting, there were already about 75 people seated.

As I sat with Ed and his staff in a small adjacent room, we could hear the noise of the crowd arriving. Ed left the room to check things out. When he returned, he asked everyone to leave except me so I could brief him once again. He was visibly excited. He told me that he had been to Preston many times and never before had he seen so many people gathered for a Labour Party meeting.

When Ed and I entered the hall, there were well over 300 people packed in. We had run out of seats. People were standing along every wall in the hall.

Just seven days before, we had only 30 committed to attend. The sole difference were the eleven leaders and good staff organizers who had known which leaders to ask to be at the center of what we were attempting to do. They had inspired eleven leaders who inspired over 300 people to turn out to the meeting.

The meeting itself was 90 minutes of high energy. Ed was great, as were all the local leaders who spoke. In fact, at one point, we asked everyone to take ten minutes, right on the spot during the meeting, to call five people they knew to get their commitment to vote Labour. The room was abuzz with over 300 times five conversations taking place almost simultaneously. The meeting ended with over 200 commitments from people to either phone call or door knock over the next seven weeks.

On the return train trip to London. Ed and his staff were as excited as I had ever seen them. Even some of the "Graf doubters" had warmed. For six weeks prior to the election, we averaged 200+ people door knocking every weekday and 400 people on the weekends.

Labour needed to go from 17 seats to 43 seats to take back the Council, and we needed to do this in a non-general election year; a result that seemed impossible. On the day of the election, our volunteers worked incredibly hard. When we gathered to get the results, we learned that we had won an astounding 39 seats. While it did not win 43 seats, Labour was now the new plurality party in Lancashire and able to put together a coalition with individual non-Tory winners to gain control of the Council. As Noel Hutchinson said, "The whole process brought a bit of magic to the campaign."

We had won an astounding 22 seats, making Labour the new plurality party.

For me, this victory was the highlight of two years' work in the UK. From there, unfortunately, my work in the UK went straight downhill.

As the general election was looming, Ed asked Douglas Alexander, an MP from Scotland, to assume the role of National Campaign Manager. From the first day I met Mr. Alexander in December of 2010, he had not agreed with my organizing approach. He did not believe that "community organizing," as he called it, could lead to a general election victory. Although we rarely met between 2011 and 2012, he continued to raise his doubts about my work. After Ed had named Alexander the National Campaign Director, he and I met briefly. He granted Labour's victory in Lancashire was wonderful, but he did not think this approach could be utilized throughout the UK.

When I told Ed of my brief meeting with Mr. Alexander, he assured me that he would work it out. While I wanted to believe Ed's assurances, I had strong doubts that he could or would do so. I continued to do training sessions for various parliamentary candidates. However, Douglas Alexander did not include me in the planning for the general election campaign. Given this, I proposed to Ed that he let me do what we had done in Lancashire in ten marginal seats leading up to the general election. Ed liked my idea and spoke to the National Campaign Manager, but my proposal never came to pass.

As time went on and nothing changed, even with Ed's assurances I became very uncertain as to what my future with the party would be. Mr. Alexander and I disagreed on too many things for it to end well for me; especially if Ed did not put his foot down, which he did not. I knew Ed well enough by this time to know that he strove to please all parties. I understood some of this was because he had many factions to deal with. However, his telling me that he needed me belied the fact that he was not clearing a path for me to really help.

One evening before I was to return to the states for a few weeks, Ed put together a surprise gathering of the staff to celebrate my 69th birthday. This was very sweet of him, but as the party broke up,

Bob Roberts, Ed's press guy, told me that in the next couple of days a story would be breaking in the news that I was working for the Labour Party as an illegal immigrant. If true, this would obviously be very embarrassing to Ed and the party.

I was stunned. I had an approved visa for the two years I had been working in the UK. Bob told me not to worry. He said it was obviously untrue and that the story would last two days and then die. He told me not to talk to the media if they contacted me. Bob told me to be proud that I had rattled the Tories so much that they had taken to pitching false stories to the press.

A few days after I arrived back in the United States, however, a story broke on the front pages of the leading Rupert Murdoch newspaper in London. On the front cover was a picture of Ed and me with the caption, "Is Ed's guru an illegal immigrant?" This was no page-six article, and the story ran for four or five days; not one or two.

Somehow the story was leaked to the press from a leading Tory blogger. Where they got the story remains a mystery. Ed assured me that Labour's attorneys would have this cleared up in a couple of weeks. But to my great dismay, this never happened. Although Ed's chief of staff stayed in contact with me, nothing changed. I was "out."

I became very frustrated with Ed Miliband. He did not personally take charge **As time** of the situation. He had arranged **passed, I** for his chief of staff to work with **moved from** Labour's attorneys and to commu- **anger and** nicate with me. Many people who **resentment** wrote to me believed that Douglas **to feeling** Alexander was the leaker. This was **grateful.** never proved, and he vehemently denied that he had anything to do with it.

Nevertheless, my time working for Labour was over. For some time, my anger and resentment focused on Ed Miliband. I had done what he had asked of me. I had spent a good deal of time in the UK, especially in 2013, away from my family. I felt he had betrayed me, as well as the Labour organizing staff I had been working with for so long.

As time passed, I moved from anger and resentment to feeling grateful for the rich experience I had working for the Labour Party in the UK and for the many lasting relationships that continue until today. I count my time and work in the UK as one of the highlights of my career.

In 2016, a year after Ed lost the general election by a wide margin, my good friend Marc Stears, then the Director of NEF (National Economic Foundation), a widely-respected policy think tank in England, asked me to come to London for a week to work with him and his staff.

I happily accepted Marc's invitation, for it not only afforded me an opportunity to work with him again but it also gave me a chance to catch up with my Labour Party friends.

When Ed heard that I was coming to London, he invited me to his home for lunch. Our time together that day, although slightly awkward, was fine. Ed wanted to apologize to me for how things had turned out. We spent about an hour together before saying goodbye. It was good to see him.

A couple of days after my visit with Ed, Marc Stears informed me that there was to be a panel discussion led by three people: Ed, the leader of the Liberal Democratic Party, and a spokeswoman from Podemos, a political party in Spain, scheduled nearby his office and he invited me to attend.

I was particularly anxious to hear from the woman from Podemos, so I went. When I arrived, I took a seat in the back corner of the room so I would not be visible to Ed or some others in the audience. At one point, someone asked Ed about the trouncing he took in the 2015 election. At the end of his answer, almost as an aside, he said that perhaps he should have listened to "Arnie Graf's advice."

I honestly do not believe that my presence would have resulted in a different outcome for Ed Miliband or the Labour Party in 2015, but as an off-the-cuff remark, it was nice to hear.

CONCLUSION

Organizing was a fulfilling career that gave me a way to combine my values and anger at injustice together into effective action. By using stories and the lessons I learned from five different organizing campaigns, I have attempted to demonstrate their universality.

I wrote this book for two primary reasons. First, I want to convey that universal organizing principles can be applied to a variety of organizational efforts, not just to organizations affiliated with the Industrial Areas Foundation (IAF).

Second, I hope my stories might encourage some people to explore organizing as a career. As a young boy born on Suffolk Street on the lower east side of Manhattan, I could never have imagined the places I've seen.

When I was eleven years old, my mother bought me a lamp with a shade that had both a map of the United States and a map of the world. I used to stare at that lamp shade every night before I went to bed. Little did I know that over the course of my lifetime I would organize in New England, the Mid-Atlantic, the Southwest, the South, and the Midwest. Nor could have I imagined myself working in the United Kingdom, Israel, Canada, and South Africa. Some of these countries, like Israel, I was in only a short time; in the UK I worked for nearly two full years. And I never thought I would be invited to South Africa with my colleague Mike Gecan to conduct organizing training sessions for 50 remarkable people from various parts of the country while the apartheid leader Frederik William DeKlerk was still the country's president.

But as interesting as the *places* I organized were, it was the *people* and the *leaders* I worked with that live on with me. Their persistence and courage always affirmed how fortunate I was to be in relationship with them. What the IAF taught me more than anything is that relational power can trump dominant power, but it takes *discipline* and *time* and *training* and, mostly especially, the *will to build it.*

To Janet Ades, my former graduate school professor and lifelong friend, thank you for introducing me to the IAF and inviting me to live an examined life that led to action.

I hope this book, for some of you readers, is your own Janet Ades.

ACKNOWLEDGMENTS

....

My life would have been very different had I not been involved as a young man with the Congress of Racial Equality (CORE) and the National Welfare Rights Organization (NWRO). These two experiences gave me an understanding that the lack of power leaves people between a rock and a hard place. With CORE, I saw what the ravages of a lack of power meant to inner city African American people. In Harlan County, Kentucky, organizing with the NWRO exposed me to what the lack of power did to retired coal miners and poor white people. These two experiences led the way into a life of organizing. They also exposed me to the importance of training and mentoring. In CORE, Al Pam gently challenged, taught, and supported me. In Harlan County, Bill Worthington mentored me. Bill is featured in the documentary, *Harlan County, USA*, an older film I still highly recommend.

When I went to the Industrial Areas Foundation Training Institute (IAF) in 1971, the associate was Dick Harmon and the director was Ed Chambers. As a trainee I was assigned to work mostly with Dick. I enjoyed him because he fired up my imagination. Most importantly, he believed in me and we remain good friends until this day. Except for my early days of organizing with Dick in Milwaukee, however, I always reported to Ed Chambers. Ed was both brilliant and brusque. I worked with him for over 40 years, and he was always there for me. While we at times disagreed on strategies or the direction about the IAF, I never doubted his support personally for me or for my family. Saul Alinsky, of course, who founded the IAF in 1940, is the one most identified with the IAF, but there would not be a modern IAF without Ed Chambers, who succeeded Alinsky after his death in 1972.

Through 43 years of working with the IAF, I have known a wide range of leaders and organizers throughout the US, Canada, South Africa, and the UK who have had a profound effect on me. I hope I haven't inadvertently left any of them out of these acknowledgments, but if I have, please forgive me.

For 40 years, Mike Gecan and I have remained close colleagues and friends. Over this period of time, we have spoken by phone 2-3 times a week. I do not know of a better organizer than Mike. He is skillful, creative, and soulful. Working with him has been one of the most joyful and important experiences of my life.

In 1994, Mike and I and some of our colleagues formed what we call "Metro IAF." Metro IAF includes

mostly the IAF organizations east of the Mississippi
River. At the same time, Ernie Cortes and Sr. Christine Stephens were organizing many of the southwest and western states under "SW/WIAF." I have
already spoken of my admiration for Ernie in chapter
two. Sr. Christine, who died in 2019, was an excellent
organizer and trainer of organizers.

After Ed Chamber's retirement in 2010 (he died
in 2015), Ernie, Sr. Christine, Mike, and I became
IAF's co-directors. None of Mike's and my plans for
building Metro IAF could have happened without
numerous others.

The Baltimoreans United in Leadership Development (BUILD) organization, as of 2020, is 44
years old. It continues to remain on the cutting edge
of change. This is due to the many talented leaders
and organizers that have worked with the organization. The base and heart of BUILD began with the
leadership of the Rev. Vernon Dobson and Ms. Mari-

an Dixon. I have spoken about Reverend Dobson and the impact he has had on my life in the chapter on BUILD. Ms. Dixon was one of the quietest yet powerful leaders that I have yet worked with. As close as I was to her, I always called her Ms. Dixon, and so I will here. As a twelve-year-old girl growing up in St. Mary's County, which is know as "the Mississippi of Maryland," Ms. Dixon was the first to integrate her Catholic Church by simply sitting in the first pew. The first time she did that, besides frightening her parents, the priest and the ushers picked her up and carried her to the back of the church. After six Sundays of doing this same exercise, the priest gave up; and after that, African Americans could sit wherever they wanted to in that church. I loved Ms. Dixon and was honored by her family when they asked me to speak at her funeral, which was packed with over one thousand people.

The undoubted political and charismatic leader of BUILD by 1981 was the Reverend Douglas Miles. He wowed the members of BUILD as a caring pastor, political strategist, and engaging preacher. The political and corporate leaders of Baltimore, seeing how important he was to BUILD's growth, tried to buy him off (as they had done with many other leaders in the past). Reverend Miles totally rejected all their offers; they had not encountered anyone like him. Bishop Miles remains a senior advisor to BUILD and my close friend to this day.

Leaders of BUILD from 1980-1984, like Carol Reckling, Irene Mallory, Catherine Brown, Pervis Bates, Harry Carpenter, Gary Rodwell, Marilyn Brooks, Wendell Wright, Father Joe Muth, Rev. Sig Arneson, and so many others infused the organization with a culture of shared leadership that set a strong foundation for the organization.

In addition to these wonderful leaders, BUILD has been fortunate to have had a number of excellent organizers. Gerald Taylor and Gary Rodwell were early lead organizers. Later, Kathleen O' Toole filled the position admirably. Kathleen took the organization through a rough time. Besides being an excellent organizer, she is a beautiful poet and person.

After Kathleen left, Jonathan Lange, became

the lead organizer. I met him in 1982 when the IAF began to work in the South with the Amalgamated Clothing and Textile Workers Union (ACTWU). Jonathan was the associate director for the southern region of the clothing and apparel division of the union. The word to describe Jonathan is "brilliant." He came to Baltimore at the invitation of BUILD to organize low wage workers. After two years, he organized the Solidarity Sponsoring Committee (SSC) that within two years, with BUILD's political help, forced the mayor and city council of Baltimore to pass the first Living Wage Law in the country in 1994. Since being BUILD's lead organizer and the founder of SSC, Jonathan has continued IAF's work with unions around the country as well as training and supervising many of IAF's newer organizers.

Rob English followed Jonathan as BUILD's next lead organizer. Rob is a special organizer and person. He has helped BUILD become as powerful as it has ever been. I worked with Rob for many years. Both of us grew from working with each other. Rob is currently the co-director of Metro IAF with Martin Trimble.

Martin Trimble came to Washington, DC, to become the first lead organizer of the Washington Interfaith Network (WIN). He took WIN from its founding to become a very significant organization in the nation's capital. Martin is currently the co-director of Metro IAF with Rob English and the co-director of the national IAF with Ernie Cortes. Martin holds these positions because he is relentless, productive, creative, and fiercely loyal.

Two of the organizers that followed Martin in DC are Amy Vruno and Jennifer Knox. Amy, who is a fine organizer, has now returned to WIN as the organization's lead organizer.

I organized WIN with a terrific core of leaders. John Moore was always there. He put as much time as anyone into organizing WIN. He teamed with Carol Wheeler, a truly beautiful person, and three terrific pastors, Revs. Darrell Macklin, Joe Daniels, and Lionel Edmonds.

Today I remain in close touch with Rev.

Edmonds. He leads, he preaches, he writes, and he is a very good musician. I love his humor and infectious laugh. He has become a wonderful friend.

Jim Drake and Lew Finfir first organized the Greater Boston Interfaith Organization (GBIO). Jim came to the IAF from Mississippi, where he had organized independent wood cutters into a strong cooperative. Prior to that, he worked for sixteen years with Cesar Chavez. Lew was very important as the co-lead organizer, as he knew people throughout the greater Boston area. Jim died too soon, on Sept. 9, 2001, and eventually Cheri Andes became the lead organizer. Cheri re-organized GBIO, broadened its base, and led the organization into a major healthcare victory when Mitt Romney was the governor of Massachusetts. Ari Lipman, a young talented organizer, assisted Cheri in organizing GBIO.

As always, as important as the organizers are, it is the leaders that make or break an organization.

GBIO was fortunate to have a wonderful mix of leaders like Fran Early, Fran Godine, Nahma Nadich, Gerry Algere, Rev. Burns Stanfield, and many others. Rabbi Jonah Pesner, who is now the director of the Religious Action Center, the social action arm of the Union of Reform Judaism, was part of this wonderful cadre of leaders.

Additionally, there were two outstanding African American pastors who added great leadership to GBIO. Rev. Ray Hammond, the pastor of Bethel AME Church, is a remarkable man. He graduated from Harvard Medical School at the age of 24 and practiced medicine for many years before becoming Bethel's full-time pastor. Rev. Hammond is strong, yet he has a calm demeanor. I miss our conversations.

When Rev. Hurman Hamilton became GBIO's president, the organization took off. I loved our early morning meetings at his favorite coffee shop, the only Black-owned coffee shop in Boston at the time. Although he is pastoring in California now, we remain good friends.

There are so many other organizers in Metro IAF today that I have decided to mention only those I have worked with directly.

Alisa Glasman did great work in Baltimore, and she is now the lead organizer in Fairfax County, Virginia. Terrell Williams is the charismatic and energetic organizer who is the co-director of Turn Around Tuesday (TAT) in Baltimore, a terrific organization that has trained and placed over 800 unemployed and returning citizens into decent paying jobs. Ojeda Phillips, while she served as BUILD's lead organizer, was one of TAT's originators. Sean Closkey is at the heart of BUILD's effort to rebuild parts of east Baltimore. To date, Rebuild Metro has rehabbed over 350 homes. There is no one more committed, smarter, or harder working than Sean.

I worked with Coleman Milling in Baltimore; Washington, DC; and Prince Georges County, Maryland. Coleman came to organizing after working for many years at a Montgomery Ward warehouse. His growth as an organizer has been a wonderful process to observe.

Larry Gordon replaced Cheri Andes as GBIO's lead organizer. I have known Larry for many years. He is a top flight organizer and is currently working with Keisha Krum and Khalilah Worley in Cleveland. I was privileged to work with Keisha in Milwaukee. You will not meet a finer person or organizer than her. I also worked with Khalilah in Cleveland. As a native of that city, she exhibits an especially strong feel for what is going on there.

Finally, I would be remiss if I did not acknowledge Bob Connolly. Simply put, there would be no IAF organization in Milwaukee if it was not for Bob.

I learned to be an organizer working for the COPS organization. It had the largest cadre of committed leaders that I had ever experienced. The leaders' devotion to the organization was palpable. Numerous leaders were buried with their COPS button. I have mentioned Fr. Al Benavides, Beatrice Gallego, Andy Sarabia, and Carmen Badillo in Chapter Two, but I would be remiss if I did not acknowledge leaders such as Beatrice Cortez, Mr. and Ms. Siller, Mr. and Mrs. Salinas, Ms. Galvan, Fr. David Garcia, Mr. and Mrs. Rueben Estrada, and Sr. Pearl Ceasar, Sr. Consuelo Tovar, and Sr. Mignonne Konecny.

One of the most moving experiences I ever had as an organizer was the two weeks I spent with my colleague Mike Gecan, training fifty civic leaders who came from all over South Africa before Nelson Mandela became the country's president, which I described in the Introduction. Although as I get older and sometimes cannot remember names and places, this experience is seared into my memory. The trainees had incredible spirit. Their singing of their national anthem was absolutely uplifting. At this training, I met and got to know Ishmael (Ish) Mkhabela. He is one of the most remarkable people I have ever met. Ish had been the head of Azapo, the organization that claimed as its roots the movement the iconic Steve Biko founded. Azapo was a militant, non-violent organization fighting to end the Apartheid regime. Ish resigned as the leader of Azapo because of his inability to stop the practice of "necklacing." If someone was suspected of treason or of being an informer, a rubber tire filled with gas was put over the person's chest and arms and set on fire. It was a horrible way to die. Ish snuck Mike and me at different times into Soweto. I will never forget the horrible choking odor from the mounds of burning garbage and the open latrines. Through Apartheid and all its horrors, however, Ish remained hopeful. I was honored when he visited my home in Maryland. After Nelson Mandela became president, he appointed Ish as his first Housing Director.

From 2011-2013, I spent a great deal of time working for the United Kingdom's Labour Party. My main man was Maurice Glassman. Maurice was responsible for bringing me to London to work with Ed Miliband, who was then the leader of the Labour party.

Besides his brilliance, Maurice has a huge heart. With him, I had more than a colleague; I developed a dear friend. I spent many Friday nights when in London at Maurice's home with his lovely wife, Catherine, and their children Harry, Thomas, Anna, and Isaac, celebrating Shabbos with a delicious meal. Tessa Jowell, MP, also became a very good friend. I loved spending the weekends with her and her family at her home in the beautiful English countryside. Tessa died too soon. I also owe a great debt of gratitude to Lina Jamoul, Jessica Jones, Bernadette Farrell, Scott Langdon, Jonathan Rutherford, and Marc Stears, for their support and friendship in my time in the UK.

I want to thank Greg Pierce of ACTA Publications, the publisher of this book. Greg edited it in a way that made my writing much better without changing any of my ideas. Every first-time author should have an editor like him. My friend Kathleen O'Toole did a great job proofreading the entire manuscript. I also want to thank Rae Cooper, who worked with me as I started out on this book, and my daughter Daisha, who typed every page.

While my friends and colleagues have been very important to my growth and work, there are no people more important to me than the family I came from, and the family I have helped form.

My father and mother came from very poor backgrounds. Dad did not finish high school, and Mom grew up living in and out of welfare. They overcame all of this to provide a very loving family to my brother, Martin—who is my dear friend—and me. We never wanted for anything, and family was central to everything that we did. We saw my grandparents, uncles, aunts, and cousins regularly. While I loved being around all of them, my best days as a kid was spent with my father watching basketball games at Madison Square Garden. Although I enjoyed basketball, the best part was spending the day with my father.

There is a line from a Rod Stewart song, "You are my lover, you are my best friend, you are in my soul." That best describes how I feel about my wife, Lucile. She is wise, loving, and beautiful. She carved out many interesting careers for herself. I would not have had the career I had, or even completed this book, without her support.

Our children Aaron, Alicia, Darrell, and Daisha are four unique people. While my wife is my soul, my children are my heart. Each has forged his or her own direction. My daughters-in-law, Miranda and Natasha, and my son-in-law, Kirby, have added to my joy.

Finally, my mother did a needlepoint picture depicting a group of children holding hands, standing in a circle. The title of the picture is, "Grandchildren Complete the Circle of Life." Thank you, Sebastian, Shiah, Ava, Phoenix, Jordan, and Laila for completing grandma and grandpa's circle of life.

COMMUNITY ORGANIZING BOOKLETS

Action Creates Public Life
Edward T. Chambers

The Body Trumps the Brain
Edward T. Chambers

Effective Organizing for Congregational Renewal
Michael Gecan

Going to the Well to Building Community
Deacon Timothy E. Tilghman

How to Raise Money for Community Organizing
Robert Connolly

Mixing It Up in the Public Arena
A. Zeik Saidman

The Power of Relational Action
Edward T. Chambers

Public Friendship
William L. Droel

Raising Money for Your Congregation
Robert Connolly

Rebuilding Our Institutions
Ernesto Cortes, Jr.

Reflecting with Scripture on Community Organizing
Reverend Jeffrey K. Krehbiel

**Using the Tools of Community Organizing to Build
Your Union's Strength in the Post-Janus Era**
Jonathan Lange, Amy Vruno, Ben Gordon

What Is Social Justice?
William L. Droel

**ACTA Publications • www.actapublications.com
800-397-2282**

BOOKS ON ORGANIZING AND SOCIAL JUSTICE

Baptized for This Moment:
Rediscovering Grace All Around Us
Stephan Paul Bouman

Going Public:
An Organizer's Guide to Citizen Action
Michael Gecan

The Heartbeat of Wounded Knee:
Native America from 1890 to Present
David Treuer

Just a Little Bit More:
The Culture of Excess and the Fate of the Common Good
T. Carlos Anderson

Lessons Learned:
Stories from a Lifetime of Organizing
Arnie Graf

People's Institutions in Decline:
Causes, Consequences, Cures
Michael Gecan

Reveille for a New Generation:
Organizers and Leaders Reflect on Power
Gregory F. Augustine Pierce, Editor

Song in a Weary Throat:
Memoir of an American Pilgrimage
Pauli Murray

The World as It Should Be:
Living Authentically in the Here-and-Now Kingdom of God
Gregory F. Augustine Pierce

ACTA Publications • www.actapublications.com
800-397-2282

charge.
- From neighborhoods, we
organize city or County wide
which allows us to
confront mayors or governors.
- Have lost connection with
neighborhood leaders.